The Civil Rights Movement for Kids

The Civil Rights Movement for Kids

A History with 21 Activities

Mary C. Turck

CHICAGO
REVIEW
PRESS

Library of Congress Cataloging-in-Publication Data

Turck, Mary C.
     Civil rights movement for kids : a history with 21 activities / Mary C. Turck.
     p. cm.
     Includes bibliographical references and index.
     Summary: Describes the struggle for civil rights for African Americans in the 1950s
and 1960s and profiles important civil rights leaders. Includes suggested activities.
     ISBN 1-55652-370-X
     1. Afro-Americans—Civil rights—History—20th century—Juvenile literature.
2. United States—Race relations—Juvenile literature. [1. Afro-Americans—Civil rights. 2. Race
relations. 3. Civil rights movement.] I. Title.

E185.61 .T925 2000
323.1´196073—dc21

                                              99-054580

Cover design: Joan Sommers Design and Paul Dolan
Interior design and illustration: Rattray Design

Front cover photographs: (clockwise) March on Washington, National Archives & Records
Administration; a civil rights march, Corbis/Bettmann; Ruby Bridges, Corbis/Bettmann.
Back cover photographs: (top) Halifax, North Carolina drinking fountain, John Vachon, Library of
Congress; Greyhound Bus waiting room sign, Library of Congress.

The author and the publisher disclaim all liability for use of the information contained in this book.

To the people of Cabrini Green, among whom I lived and from whom I learned from 1967 to 1973, and especially to Cora Williams, Excell Williams, Thelma Andrews, Angela Andrews, Mirian Crews, and the sisters, brothers, priests, and parish of St. Dominic

Contents

Acknowledgments

I would like to acknowledge a few of the important people in my life whose influence, inspiration, advice, and questions have made this a better book.

Thanks first of all to Howard and Millie Turck, my parents, and to Chuck and Helen Henrie, my uncle and aunt, whose examples and words taught me early in life to value diversity and to work for justice.

Thanks to my husband, Ron Salzberger, and to my children, Molly and Macy, for their patience with the need to sometimes subordinate family schedules to the demands of deadlines.

Thanks to Cynthia Sherry and Lisa Rosenthal, whose editing has made this a far better book! Thanks also to my agent, Jeanne Hanson, who first suggested that I write this book and then shepherded the book proposal through the acceptance process.

Finally, I wish to acknowledge my great debt to those people active in the Civil Rights Movement who made this book both possible and necessary, and especially to the often-unsung heroes and martyrs, including Daisy Bates, Septima Clark, Vernon Dahmer, Fannie Lou Hamer, Jimmy Lee Jackson, Barbara Johns, Viola Liuzzo, Chuck McDew, Diane Nash, Annell Ponder, C. T. Vivian, and many others far too numerous to list here.

Time Line

President Harry
Truman orders
integration of
armed forces

**Barbara Johns
speaks out
at Moton
High School,
asking for
equal
education**

Little Rock,
Arkansas,
schools are
integrated

Mack Parker is
lynched in
Mississippi

1948   **1951**   **1954**   **1955**   **1956**   **1957**   **1959**

Supreme Court
says no to
school
segregation
in Brown vs.
Board of
Education

**Rosa Parks
refuses to
give up her
seat on
the bus**

Montgomery bus
boycott begins

Emmett Till is
lynched

Segregation
on Alabama
buses ends by
order of the
Supreme Court

Civil Rights Act of 1964 becomes law

Marches for integration in St. Augustine, Florida

Freedom Summer education and voter registration project

Bloody Sunday in Selma, Alabama

Jimmy Lee Jackson assassinated

Reverend James Reeb assassinated

March from Selma to Montgomery, Alabama

Freedom Rides

1960   **1961**   **1962**   **1963**   **1964**   **1965**   **1966**   **1968**

Ruby Bridges begins school in New Orleans, integrating that city's elementary school system

Student sit-ins begin at Woolworth lunch counter in Greensboro, North Carolina

James Meredith integrates the University of Mississippi (Ole Miss), entering the university only under the protection of federal marshals

Birmingham crusade; police attack children with fire hoses and dogs

Birmingham church bombing; four young girls killed

Medgar Evers assassinated

March on Washington

James Chaney, Andrew Goodman, and Michael Schwerner assassinated

Mississippi Freedom Democratic Party goes to convention

Dr. Martin Luther King, Jr. wins the Nobel Peace Prize

Viola Liuzzo assassinated

Malcolm X assassinated

Voting Rights Act of 1965 becomes law

Vernon Dahmer assassinated

Dr. Martin Luther King, Jr. marches in Cicero, Illinois

Dr. Martin Luther King, Jr. assassinated

Introduction

The struggle for civil rights for African Americans exploded dramatically in the 1960s. As black children in the south faced hostile white mobs to enroll in school, the nation watched their bravery on the evening news. Television showed fire hoses turned on nonviolent demonstrators, police dogs tearing at human flesh, churches bombed, and children killed as the struggle between racism and resistance engulfed the country. The quiet heroism of black men, women, and children inspired those who watched from a distance. Soon many young people, and some who were older, streamed south to join in the civil rights struggle.

The southern Civil Rights Movement recognized its greatest leader in the Reverend Martin Luther King, Jr. Like many movement leaders, he based his commitment on his deep Christian faith. In a brilliant synthesis, Reverend King combined the nonviolent resistance tactics of Mahatma Gandhi with the prophetic Jewish cry for justice of Rabbi Abraham Heschel and his own Christian preaching on love of enemies. Even when he was beaten and jailed, his family

threatened, his home bombed, Reverend King refused to respond with violence or hatred. By the thousands, people followed his example and committed their lives to a nonviolent, loving struggle for justice. Black and white, Christian and Jewish, they found common ground in the Civil Rights Movement.

High school and college students of all races traveled south as Freedom Riders, peacefully violating law and custom as they rode side-by-side in the back and the front of Greyhound buses. Daring young people led the Student Nonviolent Coordinating Committee (SNCC) in organizing and teaching in freedom schools, in lunch counter sit-ins, and in voter registration drives.

And then the struggle moved north. In northern cities like Chicago and Milwaukee, white mobs screamed, spit, and threw rocks at peaceful marchers who sought to integrate all-white neighborhoods. Although Chicago had no laws separating white from black children in schools, residential housing segregation kept black and white families and children apart as

Daring young people led the Student Nonviolent Coordinating Committee (SNCC) in organizing and teaching in freedom schools, in lunch counter sit-ins, and in voter registration drives.

effectively as the segregation laws of Mississippi and Alabama.

In this book, children will revisit the early days of the Civil Rights Movement. Each chapter includes profiles of civil rights leaders. These profiles introduce significant women leaders like Septima Clark and Diane Nash as well as famous men of the movement. Each chapter also provides activities for children. Activities range from a Freedom Feast to a one-act play recreating a lunch counter sit-in.

Chapter One, "Let the Children Lead," describes segregation in the United States before the Civil Rights Movement. This chapter highlights the early struggle for integrated schools and introduces heroes of the movement, beginning with teenage Barbara Johns and six-year-old Ruby Bridges.

Chapter Two, "Tired of Being Mistreated," introduces Rosa Parks and Martin Luther King, Jr. The exciting success of the 1955–1956 Montgomery Bus Boycott demonstrates the success of united action and the early stages of a public mass movement.

In Chapter Three, "Nonviolent Resistance—Student Sit-Ins, 1960," young people again take center stage as they stage dramatic nonviolent protests that capture the attention of the entire world. Black college students show heroism and determination as they move into leadership roles alongside their elders.

"If Not Us, Then Who?" ask the Freedom Riders of Chapter 4. Black and white, old and young, the Freedom Riders put their lives on the line as they challenge segregation in buses, waiting rooms, and restaurants.

Chapter 5 describes people across the South "Standing Up for Freedom" from the 1963 Children's Crusade in Birmingham to Selma's Bloody Sunday in March 1965. By day, civil rights demonstrators stood up to fire hoses and police dogs, By night, civil rights leaders fell victim to midnight assassins lurking on dark streets and hiding in bushes.

In 1963, the March on Washington celebrated the Civil Rights Movement. Chapter 6, "I Have a Dream," describes the march and the steady progress of the dream of justice for all. The great march celebrated the movement and claimed its rightful place in the center of the American political scene.

Chapter 7, "Praying with My Feet," exam-

This movement is not a part of history, but a part of present-day political reality.

ines the religious roots of the Civil Rights Movement. People from diverse religious traditions came together in the movement, agreeing that each of their religions required a moral commitment to justice and equality.

Chapter 8, "You May Be Killed," focuses on the Freedom Summer of 1964. Hundreds of young men and women streamed south to work in a massive voter registration campaign. That summer had barely begun when the prophetic warning of the chapter title was tragically fulfilled for three young men in Mississippi.

Chapter 9, "The Struggle Continues," focuses on the multiple civil rights movements active at the beginning of the twenty-first century.

Although the Civil Rights Movement of the 1960s won great victories, African Americans still continue to seek an end to prejudice and discrimination based on racism. Other groups seeking justice, both in this country and around the world, have been inspired by their struggle.

Throughout this book, the Civil Rights Movement appears as a living force. This movement is not a part of history, but a part of present-day political reality. Learning about the origins of the movement sheds light on today's struggles against prejudice and discrimination. Stories of the great achievements of young people in the movement can inspire each person to care and to dare and to work for justice today.

Learning about the origins of the movement sheds light on today's struggles against prejudice and discrimination.

Let the Children Lead

Early Days, the 1950s

Introduction

Imagine laws ordering you not to eat with, ride the bus with, go to school with, or marry someone just because you and that person had different skin colors. *Segregation*, the separation of persons on the basis of skin color, was the law of the southern United States during the 1950s.

This chapter looks at segregation and the beginning of the Civil Rights Movement that ultimately dismantled segregation laws. The chapter also introduces courageous young people who dared to challenge segregation, and describes their struggles.

Legal segregation was both a product and a cause of prejudice. Prejudice means pre-judging another person or group of people, without regard to facts. For example, some adults say that young people are loud and irresponsible. That is a prejudice against all young people.

Racism is a set of prejudices against people whose skin color or ethnicity is different from your own. An *ethnic group* is a group of people who share common customs, language, values, and/or national origin.

Segregation laws were the products of prej-udice and, specifically, of racism. The laws were made by white men who believed black people were inferior. Segregation laws made it easier to be prejudiced because the law gave respectability to prejudice. These laws also increased prejudice by separating people, so that they could not get to know one another and learn about their mistaken beliefs.

Back to the 1950s

Let's take a trip back in time, back some 50 years ago. Daily life was different then, for children as well as for adults. In 1950, girls wore dresses to school and boys wore pants—but not blue jeans. Children always spoke respectfully to adults. They addressed adults by their last names—"Mr. Johnson" or "Mrs. King." Most adults also addressed each other formally, using last names. This rule of respect was broken when white adults spoke to black adults. Then the white adults usually called the black adults by their first names. Sometimes, even more dis-respectfully, they would call a black man "boy."

Fifty years ago, most mothers stayed at home. They took care of their children, homes,

Photograph by John Vachon, courtesy of Library of Congress

This drinking fountain in Halifax, North Carolina, taken in April 1938, shows the separation of black and white people in the South before the Civil Rights Movement. Black people and white people were not even allowed to drink from the same drinking fountains.

laundry, cooking, and cleaning. Women who worked outside the home had few choices. They worked at traditional "women's jobs," such as a cleaning lady or maid, office worker, teacher, librarian, or nurse. Employed women earned far less than men.

Black Americans were even more handicapped than white women in the work market. Many jobs were "for whites only." Black workers were kept in lower-paying jobs. Even if they were doing the same work as white workers, they were paid less.

Fifty years ago, there were no home computers, Internet, or video games. A new technology called television was sweeping the country. In 1946, only 6,000 television sets were manufactured. They showed only black-and-white images. By 1953, factories churned out seven million sets. Color had been introduced, though most televisions and most programs were still black-and-white. Parents worried that children spent more time in front of the television than they did on school and homework.

In 1950, there was not a single McDonald's restaurant in the United States. The first golden arches were built in Chicago in 1955. Rock and roll music began with Elvis Presley in the 1950s. Adults worried that his wild dancing and music would corrupt children.

Barbie was introduced in 1959. More than 200 million Barbie dolls were sold in the next 25 years. Like all other dolls on the market, Barbie was white. Black girls found no dolls that looked like them.

From 1948 to 1952, Harry Truman was president of the United States. Dwight D. Eisenhower followed him, serving from 1952 to 1960. People in the United States were deeply afraid of communism. Many people were fired from their jobs because they were suspected of being communists.

Segregation

Fifty years ago, all across the United States, black people and white people were segregated. Their homes, schools, churches, and social lives were completely separated from one another. Where there were large numbers of Mexican Americans or American Indians, they were also segregated from white people.

In the southern United States, segregation was actually the law. Throughout the South, the law forbade black people from eating in the same restaurants as white people. Black men and women taking the bus to work had to sit in the back. White people sat in the front. Even before they started school, black children learned that they were not allowed to use "white" drinking fountains or "white" bathrooms in gas stations. Black teens could not swim in public swimming pools or at public

The Red Scare

Communism is a political and economic theory that says the government should control the means of production and all people should share equally in economic well-being. In practice, the communist government of the Soviet Union was brutal to its own people and hostile to the United States. During the 1940s and 1950s, many people feared that communists would try to violently overthrow the government of the United States.

beaches reserved for whites. Even in old age, segregation separated senior citizens. The law made it a crime for an old black man and an old white man to play checkers together in the park.

In the northern United States, the laws usually did not require segregation. Even without such laws, people's lives were segregated. People of color were not allowed to buy or rent homes in the same neighborhoods as white people. Because they lived in segregated neighborhoods, children attended mostly-white or mostly-black schools.

In the North as well as in the South, employers used color as a reason for hiring or not

Fifty years ago, Black Americans were even more handicapped than white women in the work market.

hiring people. For example, most northern police forces and fire departments refused to hire any people of color.

Young people went to strictly segregated dances and social events. Friendships between black and white teens were forbidden by their elders. In many states, the law itself forbade marriage between black people and white people.

In the South, children attended strictly segregated schools from kindergarten on. Black schools got far less money than white schools. They had fewer books and worse buildings and playgrounds, if they had playgrounds at all. Teachers in black schools were paid less than teachers in white schools. The same school boards—made up of white men—ruled over black and white schools in each county.

Black parents and children protested against this inequality. They knew that segregation was legal. The Supreme Court, which makes the final judgment on whether laws passed by Congress or the states are constitutional, had said that segregation was legal as long as the segregated facilities were "separate but equal."

Black parents and children knew that their schools were anything but equal. They also knew it was dangerous to challenge the white people who ran the government. In South Carolina, Reverend J.A. DeLaine tried to get better education for black children. He and his wife and two sisters and a niece were all fired from their jobs. His house was burned to the ground while the fire department watched. His church was stoned. He was threatened with death and survived shotguns fired at him in the night. Finally, he had to flee the town where he had lived his whole life.

Other black people who challenged white power were lynched. When a mob kills someone without due process of law, it is called *lynching*. Black soldiers, returned from fighting for freedom and democracy during World War II, sometimes objected to being second-class citizens at home. Many were lynched by white mobs. During three weeks of the summer of 1946, six black war veterans were lynched in Georgia.

Despite the danger, some black and white people joined together to work for civil rights for black people. They formed the National Association for the Advancement of Colored People, the oldest and largest civil rights organization in the United States. The NAACP was

Black people were required to use separate doors and seating areas in restaurants or cafes as this 1940 photograph from Durham, North Carolina, shows. Often, they could purchase food but had to take it outside the restaurant to eat.

The Separate but Equal Doctrine

Segregation of public facilities, including schools, was upheld by the Supreme Court in 1896 in a case called Plessy versus Ferguson. The court said: "Laws permitting, or even requiring, separation . . . do not necessarily imply the inferiority of either race to the other . . ." The court went on to say: "We consider the underlying fallacy of the plaintiff's argument to consist in the assumption that the enforced separation of the two races stamps the colored race with a badge of inferiority. If this be so, it is not by reason of anything found in the act, but solely because the colored race chooses to put that construction upon it."

organized in 1909, after rioting whites in Atlanta, Georgia, killed nearly 50 black people in three days in 1906.

The NAACP's Web site (www.naacp.org/) states the purpose of the organization:

> The principal objective of the NAACP is to ensure the political, educational, social and economic equality of minority group citizens of the United States.

> The NAACP is committed to achievement through non-violence and relies upon the press, the petition, the ballot, and the courts, and is persistent in the use of legal and moral persuasion even in the face of overt and violent racial hostility.

Many southerners hated the NAACP and considered it a "subversive" or "communist" organization. Many times, NAACP members in the South were threatened or beaten. Despite the danger, the NAACP continued its activities. During the late 1940s, NAACP lawyers filed lawsuits challenging segregated, unequal education in the South. One of these lawsuits began in 1947, in Prince Edward County, Virginia.

Barbara Johns Speaks Out

In 1947, black students attended Moton High School in the town of Farmville in Prince Edward County, Virginia. Moton did not have enough room for its black students. The county government built three tar-paper shacks as temporary classrooms. The shacks had no real walls, only wooden structures covered by a heavy, black paper.

Moton High School's history teacher had to

drive the school bus, too. His other duties included building wood fires in the tar-paper shacks to heat them. The wood fires didn't keep students warm. All through the winter, they studied wearing their coats.

Moton High School had no cafeteria and no lockers. Its science classes did not have even a single microscope. The buses that brought students to school were hand-me-downs given to Moton by the white high school when it got new buses. Black parents asked for new schools. The county promised the black principal a new school, but it never kept this promise.

In the spring of 1951, Barbara Johns was a 16-year-old junior in high school. Johns was a student council member, as was her brother John. Johns had had enough of hand-me-down buses and ramshackle schools. She talked to her brother and to student council president Carrie Stokes and a few other students. Johns knew that action was difficult and dangerous. She and her friends met in secret. They gathered support slowly, and did not tell any adults of their plans.

Johns said that since their elders had not been able to get a decent school, it was time for teens to take action. She told her friends that

Changes in Reference

In 1909, the terms "black" and "Negro" were not considered dignified. They were terms used by slave traders and slave owners. Besides, many people of color are light-skinned, not black. At that time, "colored" was a respectful term.

Later, "Negro" became the term preferred by black people for decades. During the 1960s, "black" became the preferred term. Some people, like long-time civil rights leader Roy Wilkins, continued to prefer the term "Negro," and refused to change. In the 1990s, many black people adopted "African American" as their identity. They said that this name more accurately reflects their heritage and ancestry.

they would not get a new school for themselves because change would take a long time. Maybe, Johns said, they could get a decent school for their little brothers and sisters.

On April 23, Johns and her classmates set their plans in action. They faked an emergency telephone call to the principal. He left the building to attend to the "emergency." Then they delivered notes "from the principal" calling all classes to a general assembly.

The 450 students and their teachers arrived in the auditorium. Johns stood up in front of

The NAACP was organized in 1909, after rioting whites in Atlanta, Georgia, killed nearly 50 black people in three days in 1906.

Johns said that since their elders had not been able to get a decent school, it was time for teens to take action.

the assembly. She announced that this was a special meeting to discuss school conditions. Teachers protested and tried to stop the meeting. Johns took her shoe off and pounded it like a gavel. She ordered teachers to leave and her friends escorted them out of the auditorium.

The students listened to Johns's call for a decent school. They considered her explanation that it was up to them to act. They knew that they were entitled to an equal education. They knew that they should not have to go to class in tar-paper shacks. They also knew the dangers of demanding anything from the white people who ran the county government. They thought about the danger they would face if they took action and the injustice that they suffered so long as no one acted. Then all 450 students followed Johns out of school and on strike.

Johns and her group summoned lawyers from the NAACP. The lawyers thought they would be meeting with adults—they did not want to meet with children. They arrived in town in time to speak to a mass meeting attended by a thousand people. The NAACP lawyers explained that they could not help Johns and her community to get a new, but

equal, segregated school. They wanted to do something even more radical than Johns had planned. The NAACP lawyers would sue for integrated schools for all the black and white children of Farmville!

Integration! Integration meant an end to segregation, the separation of people by skin color. Integration was beyond Johns's dreams, but she and the other students and their parents agreed. The NAACP lawyers filed a lawsuit. The Moton High School case was joined with lawsuits from other towns, including one filed in Topeka, Kansas.

In Topeka, a young girl named Linda Brown attended a black elementary school. She had to travel more than two miles to the segregated school. A white school was just four blocks from her home. Linda and her parents believed that she should be able to attend the school closest to her home. They agreed to become part of the NAACP's legal challenge to segregation.

Three years later, the NAACP lawsuits finally reached the Supreme Court of the United States. By now the case was named Brown v. Board of Education. In 1954, the Supreme Court ruled that school segregation violated the

Constitution of the United States. Separate schools were inherently unequal. The highest court in the country ordered that all public schools be integrated.

What happened to Johns while the law took its slow course? A few days after the student strike, the Ku Klux Klan burned a cross in her family's front yard. The Klan is an organization based on hatred of black people. The Klan also hates other people of color as well as Jews and Catholics. Cross-burnings are warnings that the Klan is ready to attack. Johns's parents hurried her out of town. They sent her to live with an uncle in Montgomery, Alabama.

Did Johns's organizing and protest win a victory? Yes, but that victory was a long time coming. Even after the 1954 Supreme Court decision, Prince Edward County refused to integrate its schools. Instead, public officials closed all the public schools for five years. White children attended private schools. Black children had no schools.

Across the South, school boards and government officials delayed desegregation. Black parents and children, helped by the NAACP, kept up steady pressure. Throughout the years of struggle, brave children carried the burden of grown-up hatred.

Ruby Bridges Goes to School

Ruby Bridges, age six, was the first black child to attend a previously all-white school in New Orleans in 1960. Bridges grew up in Louisiana. She had seven brothers and sisters. In 1960, school integration overshadowed their lives.

Bridges's father, Abon Bridges, did not want her to integrate the William Frantz Grade School. He feared for her future. Her mother, Lucille, insisted that Ruby must do it. Lucille Bridges wanted a better education for all her children.

In a conversation with a television reporter years later, Bridges remembered her first day of school.

That first morning I remember mom saying as I got dressed in my new outfit, "Now, I want you to behave yourself today, Ruby, and don't be afraid. There might be a lot of people outside this new school, but I'll be with you." That conversation was the full

Linda Brown attended a black elementary school. She had to travel more than two miles to the segregated school. A white school was just four blocks from her home.

Throughout the years of struggle, brave children carried the burden of grown-up hatred.

extent of preparing me for what was to come.

Four federal marshals came to take Bridges to school that day. The federal marshals were there to enforce the law, because the local police would not. They walked Bridges through the crowds of white men and women. Grown men and women threw things and screamed insults at Bridges.

Bridges walked through the mob of people. She was not hit by any of the things they threw. Inside the school, she found herself in a classroom all alone with a teacher. All the white parents had kept their children home from school. Only one teacher, a woman who had just arrived from Boston, agreed to teach Bridges.

Every day, Bridges and the four marshals went to the school. Every day they met angry mobs. "Two, four, six, eight, we don't want to integrate," chanted the white adults. They kept white children out of the school for more than a year.

Looking back, Bridges calls her mother a hero.

I was a six-year-old child. I'm a parent now. I'm an adult. I believe that it took more strength and courage for my mother, my parents, to go through that than it did for me as a six-year-old. I was actually doing what I was told. . . . But for an adult to say that this is something that I will subject my six-year-old to, that takes a lot of courage and a lot of strength.

The whole family needed strength. Because Bridges was going to a white school, her father was fired from his job. Her grandparents were evicted from the farm where they had lived and worked for 25 years.

Bridges and her family persevered. Every day Bridges prayed for her tormentors. Eventually the angry crowds went away. White parents saw their children sitting at home and learning nothing. One by one, they decided that education was more important than segregation. Slowly, the white children came back to school. Finally, Bridges's school room filled up with classmates instead of empty desks.

Now a grown woman with four children of her own, Bridges continues to work for education, children, and families. She tells people that, "It is now a time for us to be concerned with all children, not just our own. We must become mother and father to all children for a better world."

A Hard-Won Victory

Schools were a very important part of the Civil Rights Movement. The legal challenges to school segregation mounted by the NAACP succeeded in overturning the "separate but equal" doctrine. In 1954, the Supreme Court ruled that racially segregated schools were unequal and unconstitutional.

Corbis/Bettmann

Six-year-old Ruby Bridges showed courage when she integrated an elementary school in New Orleans in 1960.

Roy Wilkins

Roy Wilkins, the grandson of slaves, was born in St. Louis on August 30, 1901. He was raised by an aunt and uncle in Duluth, Minnesota, after his mother died. His uncle worked as a butler for the president of the Northern Pacific Railroad.

Roy Wilkins attended integrated grade schools and high schools and the University of Minnesota. Then Wilkins became a newspaper editor at the *Kansas City Call*. Later, Wilkins moved to New York to work on *The Crisis*, the newspaper of the NAACP. From then on, Wilkins spent his life working for the NAACP. He committed his whole life to working for an end to segregation.

In 1934, Wilkins marched in Washington, D.C. to protest the failure of the Attorney General to give due emphasis to the crime of lynching. During this protest, Wilkins was arrested for the first time.

Wilkins became executive secretary of the NAACP in 1955. He chaired the Leadership Conference on Civil Rights for many years. He died in 1981 at the age of 80. He had served for 22 years as the executive secretary of the NAACP.

Adults, lawyers, and courts were important in overturning legal segregation of schools. But their action alone was not enough. The courage and commitment of young people like Barbara Johns and Ruby Bridges were needed to make civil rights a reality in the nation's schools.

Schools were just one of the battlegrounds of the Civil Rights Movement. Soon the eyes of the nation focused on the struggle to integrate public transportation in Montgomery, Alabama.

Starting Somewhere Survey

When U.S. marshals honored Ruby Bridges at a ceremony celebrating Black History Month in 1996, she said, "I wish there were enough marshals to walk with every child as they face the hatred and racism today, and to support and encourage them the way these federal marshals did for me."

Do you know what hatred and racism Ruby Bridges was talking about? Do you see separation of people of different skin colors in your town or school today? Do you see racism at work in your community? What are some examples of racism or separation that you have observed? What can you do in the continuing fight against hatred and racism?

Directions

Begin by making copies of the Starting Somewhere Survey. First, fill out the survey yourself. Then, ask a good friend or close relative to fill it out. Share the stories and questions from your surveys with each other.

Continue asking other people to fill out the survey and sharing the results, stories, and questions. When reviewing all your collected surveys, do you notice any patterns? How are people's answers similar? How are they different?

Starting Somewhere Survey

A wise person once said that the first step on a journey is the hardest. The first step on the journey to ending racism is different for each person. One good step is to begin understanding your own attitudes toward skin color and where these attitudes began. Another good step is to begin talking about race and racism with people whose skin color is different from your own. The Starting Somewhere Survey is designed to help people look at their own attitudes toward race and to begin conversations with others.

1. Think back and remember the first time that you noticed people have different skin colors. Write down that memory.

   _____

   _____

   _____

2. Do you have friends of different skin colors?   ❑ Yes   ❑ No

   List your three best friends who have different skin colors:

   _____

   _____

   _____

   _____

3. Would you be comfortable talking with your friends about skin color and about what it means in their daily lives? Why or why not?

   _____

   _____

   _____

   _____

4. List three questions that you would like to ask someone of a different skin color:

   _____

   _____

   _____

   _____

   _____

The Civil Rights Movement for Kids, © 2000. Published by Chicago Review Press, Inc. 800-888-4741.

Plan a Civil Rights Event

Y ou can organize a civil rights activity that involves your whole class—or even your whole school! You will learn about organizing as well as about civil rights.

Materials

Paper

Pen or pencil

Directions

First, make a list of people who might help you. These people may be your friends, teachers, or other adults in your school or community.

Second, talk to each person on your list and ask whether he or she is willing to help you organize a Civil Rights Week.

Third, call a meeting of the people who want to work together. At your meeting, decide when your project will take place and whether it will involve one or more classrooms or the whole school. Figure out who needs to be contacted for permission. Assign volunteers to

Join Up!

When Barbara Johns began organizing her high school, she looked for other people who were also committed to getting a better school. Do you know other people who are interested in civil rights and who would like to join together to work for an end to racism? Maybe you could start your own group in your community or school. Or you could join a group that already exists.

Many of the young people in the Civil Rights Movement began by joining a local NAACP Youth Council. One place that you can get information about existing groups is the NAACP Youth and College Division, 4805 Mount Hope Drive, Manassas, VA 22110, telephone (703) 368-4214.

You can also look for groups on-line. Try these addresses as a beginning:

Human Rights Web   www.hrweb.org/

Youth Peace   www.nonviolence.org

handle publicity through announcements and posters. Choose the activities you will include. Here are some suggestions.

- Invite a special speaker to your class or to an all-school assembly

- Choose books such as *Ruby Bridges* by Robert Coles that older students can read to kindergarten, first- or second-grade classes

- Sponsor a civil rights poster contest

- Show videos about civil rights in class (see Additional Resources at the end of this book for suggested videos)

Civil Rights Team Project

In 1996, the Maine Attorney General Andrew Ketterer began the Civil Rights Teams Project in 18 high schools and middle schools. Attorney General Ketterer was concerned because of the increasing number of teenagers charged with violent acts and threats based on prejudice. In most cases, said the attorney general's office, "the serious violence was preceded by months, and sometimes years, of a lower level of harassment generally beginning with the use of the language of hate."

Think about it: Have you ever heard racist name-calling in your school? Have you heard hate language or witnessed harassment? Could your school use a Civil Rights Team to improve the atmosphere?

In Maine, the Civil Rights Teams were made up of three students from each grade and one or two faculty advisors, all trained by the attorney general's office and assisted by a community advisor to attend some meetings, provide information and resources, and help the teams address problems of prejudice and harassment.

Some of the projects that Civil Rights Teams worked on were:

Sponsoring a Civil Rights Week, with a variety of activities for the whole school

Producing civil rights public service announcements regarding respect and tolerance, to be read over the school radio or during daily announcements

Starting a Diversity Issues Book Club, to read and discuss books such as *The Children* by David Halberstam

Decorating bulletin boards with a civil rights theme

Hosting a movie party featuring a film about racism

Making educational posters to teach lessons about the destructiveness of racial hatred

If you would like to find out more about Civil Rights Teams, visit the Civil Rights Team Web page at www.state.me.us/ag/links.htm.

2

Tired of Being Mistreated

Montgomery
Bus Boycott,
1955-56

Tired of Being Mistreated

Introduction

In 1955, most black people in Montgomery, Alabama, rode public buses every day. They rode buses from their homes in the black section of Montgomery to their jobs in the white section of Montgomery. They paid 30,000 to 40,000 bus fares each day. White people rode the buses, too, but more white people drove cars.

Segregation laws reserved the front seats in city buses for white people. In between the black section and the white section lay "no-man's-land." This section consisted of several rows of seats that were claimed by whoever got on the bus first.

Segregated buses were a daily insult and inconvenience to black men and women. In Montgomery, the civil rights struggle sprang to life in the interior of these buses.

Claudette Colvin

On March 2, 1955, Claudette Colvin said "No" to segregation and went to jail for her defiance. When she was arrested, Colvin was a high school student in Montgomery, Alabama. She went to jail because she refused to obey the segregation laws.

Like all black people in Montgomery, Colvin understood the segregation laws. She knew that the laws ordered black people to sit in the back of the bus. When Colvin boarded the bus, the black section was full. So she sat down in "no-man's-land," along with three other black women. Gradually, the white section of the bus filled up, too. At the Court Street stop, a few white people got on the bus. The driver ordered the four black women sitting in "no-man's-land" to move to the back of the bus.

Two of the women gave up their seats. Since there were no empty seats in the black section, they stood in the aisle in the back of the bus.

Colvin and another woman refused to move to the back of the bus. The driver called the police. Then a black man in the back offered his seat to the older woman. She moved to the back. Only Colvin still sat, defiantly, in "no-man's-land."

Colvin argued with the police and the white passengers. She got madder by the minute. She swore at the police and started to cry.

Segregated buses were a daily insult and inconvenience to black men and women.

21

When she was arrested, Colvin was a high school student in Montgomery, Alabama. She went to jail because she refused to obey the segregation laws.

Eventually the police dragged her off the bus. Colvin screamed in anger and frustration as they handcuffed her and took her to jail. Colvin was not the first black person to be arrested because of the bus segregation laws. She would not be the last.

Fred Gray was a young black lawyer and preacher in Montgomery. He was eager to represent Claudette Colvin. Gray wanted to use her case to challenge the legality of segregation. Many people in Montgomery's African American community agreed with him. So did Colvin. She was brave and ready to face the danger of fighting segregation.

Most of the witnesses on the bus were frightened. They feared going to court to testify. If they testified, they might lose their jobs. They might be evicted from their houses. They might even be beaten or shot at by angry white people.

The judge knew that Fred Gray wanted to challenge segregation. He decided to make it easier for Claudette Colvin to give up than to challenge segregation. He sentenced Colvin only to pay a small fine.

Colvin was ready to refuse to pay the fine and to appeal to a higher court. Then Colvin's lawyer and supporters found out that she was pregnant. They decided that the legal challenge would have to wait. She was too young and vulnerable to bear the burden of the challenge. Her family agreed and paid the fine. Uneasily, the African American community of Montgomery settled back to wait for a better opportunity to challenge segregation. They would not have to wait long.

Rosa Parks Refuses

On December 1, 1955, Rosa Parks started on her way home. Like Claudette Colvin, she found the back section of the bus full and sat down in "no-man's-land." As the bus filled up, the driver ordered her to move to the back. Rosa Parks refused.

Rosa Parks was a 42-year-old seamstress and housekeeper. Her husband, Raymond Parks, was a barber. Some have described Rosa Parks as a quiet, soft-spoken working woman. She was all of that, and much more. Along with her husband, she was a leader in the local NAACP. She had studied nonviolence and organizing tactics at the Highlander Folk School in Tennessee.

Rosa Parks was arrested and fingerprinted when she refused to give up her seat on the bus.

Rosa Parks was ready to act. She knew Claudette Colvin and she knew all about Colvin's arrest. She knew that she, too, would be arrested. She knew that she would go to jail. And she was ready to make a test case that would challenge the segregation laws of Montgomery, Alabama. She couldn't have known it at the time, but her challenge would change the country forever.

In later years, many people said Rosa Parks refused to give up her seat because she had worked hard all day and was tired. That wasn't her own explanation. In her book *Rosa Parks: My Story*, Parks explains, "I was not tired physically, or no more tired than I usually was at the end of a working day. I was not old, although some people have an image of me as being old then. I was forty-two. No, the only tired I was, was tired of giving in."

Rosa Parks was arrested and jailed. She was allowed to call home. Her mother quickly contacted civil rights leader E. D. Nixon. Nixon knew that jail meant danger for black people. Black people were often harassed in jail, sometimes beaten or abused. With the help of friends, Nixon posted bond so Parks could be released pending trial. Back at the Parks home, Nixon asked Parks whether she would be willing to make her case a battle against segregation. Would she be willing to take the case all the way to the Supreme Court?

"I was not tired physically, or no more tired than I usually was at the end of a working day. . . . No, the only tired I was, was tired of giving in."

The Highlander Folk School

Advocating racial equality and democracy, the Highlander Folk School taught leadership skills to thousands of blacks and whites. People of all colors mingled freely in its faculty and students. It had been founded by Myles Horton in 1932. Horton, a white man, had been a theology student and his commitment to equality and democracy was based in his Christian religious beliefs.

During the 1950s, Highlander's Citizenship Schools taught black people in the South to read and write. Once these skills were learned, they could register to vote.

Enemies of Highlander called it a communist school. Later, some people applied this same label to the whole Civil Rights Movement. Southern courts shut down the Highlander Folk School in 1960. It reopened as the Highlander Research and Education Center.

At Highlander's 40th anniversary celebration, Horton set out the philosophy of the school. "We believe that education leads to action," he said. "If you advocate just one action, you're an organizer. We teach leadership here. Then people go out and do what they want."

Everyone knew that this was a question for the whole Parks family to decide. If Rosa challenged the segregation law, she would be under attack by the white establishment. So would her relatives. They would lose jobs, farms, and homes. Rosa Parks talked with her husband and family long into the night. With their support and approval she decided to go ahead.

Black women professors at Alabama State University had organized the Women's Political Council. They knew Rosa Parks through civil rights work. The professors met secretly at the University at midnight. They wrote and rewrote a letter of protest. In part, the letter read:

> *Another Negro woman has been arrested and thrown into jail because she refused to get up out of her seat on the bus and give it to a white person. . . . Until we do something to stop these arrests, they will continue. The next time it may be you, or you or you. This woman's case will come up Monday. We are, therefore, asking every Negro to stay off the buses on Monday in protest of the arrest and trial.*

The professors worked quickly and quietly through the night. They made thousands of copies of the letter and prepared to distribute it. The next day was Friday. About 50 leaders assembled in a church basement. The church was Reverend Martin Luther King, Jr.'s Dexter Avenue Baptist Church. The church leaders drafted another leaflet. They used many of the women's eloquent words. Their leaflet called on supporters to come to a mass meeting on Monday night at the Holt Street Baptist Church.

Both the professors' leaflet and the ministers' leaflet were distributed widely throughout Montgomery's black community. Many leaflets were distributed through churches. On Sunday morning, many of the black ministers in Montgomery called on their congregations to observe the bus boycott. One white minister joined in their call.

On Monday morning, many black people in Montgomery walked to work. Others shared rides, or waited at bus stops for the black-owned cabs to pick them up. The city sent police on motorcycles to escort the almost-empty buses. Some black people who had not heard about the boycott were scared away by the police presence. No black people rode the buses.

Down at the courthouse, Rosa Parks went to trial. She was found guilty of breaking the segregation law. She was fined $14. Her lawyers got ready to file the appeal that would take her case to higher courts. No matter how small the fine, the principle remained the same. This time, they would not back down.

Who Was Rosa Parks?

Rosa McCauley was born in Tuskegee, Alabama, on February 4, 1916. She was the daughter of a carpenter and a teacher and the great-granddaughter of slaves and indentured servants. When she was six years old, she lay awake at night as her grandfather sat up with a shotgun. He watched and waited, ready to protect the family from the Ku Klux Klan.

Parks loved learning. She went to school all that she could, even when she had to walk eight miles to get there. She also worked hard, sometimes picking cotton in the fields near her home. After sixth grade, there were no more schools for black children near her home. Her mother sent her to Montgomery. In Montgomery, she attended a private school for black children run by some white women from the North. Parks worked at the school to help pay her tuition. She swept floors, dusted desks, emptied wastebaskets, and cleaned blackboards.

"Another Negro woman has been arrested and thrown into jail because she refused to get up out of her seat on the bus and give it to a white person. . . . We are, therefore, asking every Negro to stay off the buses on Monday in protest of the arrest and trial."

The Montgomery Advertiser was not sympathetic to the bus boycott. Once the story became the biggest news in town, the newspaper had to report on the boycott.

Parks got partway through college. Then she had to drop out to take care of her sick grandmother and, later, her sick mother. She finished school after her marriage to Raymond Parks. Her husband was a black barber working in Montgomery. Raymond was active in the NAACP and in other civil rights work. Rosa became his enthusiastic partner in his civil rights work.

After the Montgomery bus boycott, both Rosa and Raymond Parks remained active in the Civil Rights Movement. They moved to Detroit and lived there the rest of their lives. Raymond died in 1977. Rosa Parks, the "Mother of the Civil Rights Movement," still lived in Detroit at the time of the writing of this book.

"People Get Tired"

On the following Monday, Rosa Parks spent her day at the courthouse while a group of black ministers got together. They discussed plans for the mass meeting planned for that evening. They debated whether to keep the names of leaders secret to avoid danger from white people. Arriving late, Reverend Martin Luther King,

Jr. walked in on this argument. He said he was no coward—he would stand behind his actions and wanted all the other leaders to do the same.

The ministers agreed to form the Montgomery Improvement Association (M.I.A.) to coordinate the boycott and elected Reverend Martin Luther King, Jr. as president of the association. They prepared for that night's protest meeting.

Monday night, people walked to the mass meeting. The crowd continued to grow until it filled the church and hundreds more stood outside. Those outside listened attentively as the meeting was broadcast on loudspeakers. From *Eyes on the Prize* we can hear Dr. King's words as he addressed the crowd:

There comes a time that people get tired. We are here this evening to say to those who have mistreated us so long that we are tired—tired of being segregated and humiliated; tired of being kicked about by the brutal feet of oppression . . . [I]f you will protest courageously and yet with dignity and Christian love, when the history books are written in future generations, the historians

"We are here this evening to say to those who have mistreated us so long that we are tired— tired of being segregated and humiliated; tired of being kicked about by the brutal feet of oppression."

will pause and say, "There lived a great people—a black people—who injected new meaning and dignity into the veins of civilization." That is our challenge and our overwhelming responsibility. (Eyes on the Prize, p. 76)

At the start of the boycott, the M.I.A. made three demands to the city and its bus company. They asked for courteous treatment on the buses. They asked for first-come, first-served seating with whites in front and blacks in back. Finally, they asked that the bus company hire black drivers for black bus routes. (At that time, there were no black bus drivers in Montgomery.) The bus company and the city commissioners refused to consider their demands. And the boycott went on.

Many black people, including Rosa Parks, were fired from their jobs for participating in the boycott. Others were arrested as they stood on street corners waiting for rides. Police charged them with being a "public nuisance."

Boycott leaders, including Rosa Parks and Dr. King, were arrested and charged with lead-

ing an illegal action. Some boycott leaders, like Dr. King, had their homes bombed.

For the next 381 days, black people walked, shared rides, or stayed home. At the end of the year the M.I.A. called on black people to restore the true meaning of Christmas and not buy gifts. Instead, they should take the money that they would have spent on gifts and save some, give some to charity, and give some to the M.I.A. People agreed. Downtown city merchants felt the pinch in their profits. Since most bus passengers had been black people, the bus company lost money and, by the beginning of 1956, faced bankruptcy. The company wanted the boycott to end.

The black people of Montgomery persevered, with patience and courage. They made their case in the streets as their lawyers made their case in the courts. Finally, more than a year after Rosa Parks's arrest, the case reached the Supreme Court of the United States. The Supreme Court ruled that the segregation of buses was unconstitutional. On December 21, 1956, the black people of Montgomery got back on the buses, and they sat down anywhere they liked.

For the next 381 days, black people walked, shared rides, or stayed home.

A Leader Emerges

A new leader, Martin Luther King, Jr., emerged from the Montgomery bus boycott. He was a young man, only 26 years old. He had moved to Montgomery to become pastor of Dexter Avenue Baptist Church only a year before the boycott began. He would live less than 12 more years after it ended.

Martin Luther King, Jr. was born in Atlanta on January 15, 1929. He was the son of a young Baptist minister. King's mother was the daughter and granddaughter of ministers. He was named Michael after his father. When he was only five years old, his father changed both their names to Martin Luther, in honor of Martin Luther, the founder of Protestant Christianity.

Young Martin grew up during the Depression. As a small child, he watched long lines of hungry people stretch down whole blocks and around corners in his neighborhood. The lines were full of jobless people waiting for food hand-outs. Their poverty and desperation made a lasting impression on young Martin.

As a boy, Martin longed to be a leader. He begged his way into school early, starting along with his one-year-older sister Christine. When the teacher discovered that Martin was only five years old, she sent him home. Returning the following year, Martin skipped grades in a vain effort to keep up with Christine, who also skipped grades.

Martin Luther King, Jr. considered becoming a doctor or lawyer. He finally followed in his father's footsteps into the ministry. He enjoyed his college and seminary years, made many friends, and learned to play pool. More importantly, King also threw himself into the study of Social Gospel. The Social Gospel teaches that Christians must dedicate themselves to the social as well as spiritual welfare of humankind. In college, he met, courted, and married a talented young classical music singer, Coretta Scott.

As a young minister, King quickly became the foremost leader of the Civil Rights Movement. His wife and young family suffered with him through his arrests and imprisonments. They endured bombings of their home and

On December 21, 1956, the black people of Montgomery got back on the buses, and they sat down anywhere they liked.

A new leader,
Martin Luther King,
Jr., emerged from
the Montgomery bus
boycott.

threats to all their lives. With him, they committed themselves to the cause of justice and equal rights for all—black and white and brown, poor and rich, powerless as well as powerful.

Despite his youth, King spoke with authority and eloquence. His leadership of the Civil Rights Movement was acknowledged around the world in 1964, when he was awarded the Nobel Peace Prize. As he gained international recognition, King also spoke about international issues. He called for economic sanctions against South Africa, where apartheid gave a white minority absolute power over the black majority.

Keeping the Victory

The bus boycott ended when Montgomery's buses were integrated, but integration did not come easily. Angry whites attacked and beat a 15-year-old Negro girl standing at a bus stop. Others shot into buses, on one occasion shooting a pregnant Negro woman.

With the success of the bus boycott, the Civil Rights Movement picked up momentum.

Dr. Martin Luther King, Jr. sent out invitations to ministers to come to a Negro Leaders

Corbis/Flip Schulke

Martin Luther King, Jr. was a father as well as a minister and a leader of the Civil Rights Movement.

Conference on Nonviolent Integration in January 1957. As the conference was about to open in Atlanta, bombs hit the homes of church and civil rights leaders around Montgomery. The ministers at the conference founded a new organization and elected King as its president. The new organization eventually became the Southern Christian Leadership Conference (SCLC).

King led the SCLC through 11 tumultuous years, until he was assassinated in Memphis, Tennessee, in 1968. Under his leadership, the SCLC led a movement of nonviolent resistance to segregation. Nonviolent civil disobedience to unjust laws became the hallmark of the Civil Rights Movement.

After King's death in 1968, SCLC co-founder Reverend Ralph Abernathy took over as head of the SCLC. He was followed by the Reverend Joseph Lowery in 1977. In 1997, Martin Luther King III was elected president of the SCLC.

The Montgomery bus boycott had tested and proven both the effectiveness of nonviolence and the strength of its young leader, Dr. Martin Luther King, Jr. More challenges lay ahead. The nonviolent direct action of the Civil Rights Movement began to spread across the South.

King's leadership of the Civil Rights Movement was acknowledged around the world in 1964, when he was awarded the Nobel Peace Prize.

Workshop on Nonviolence

In this activity, you will learn about the principles of nonviolence and discuss how they apply in your own time and place in history.

Materials

Copier

5-by-7 index cards

Tape

Directions

Before you begin the workshop, make copies of the "Introduction to Nonviolence" for all participants.

Introduction to Nonviolence

Mohandas (Mahatma) Gandhi (1869–1948) used nonviolent demonstrations and nonviolent resistance to win India's independence from Britain in 1947. Dr. Martin Luther King, Jr. believed strongly in nonviolence. He led the Civil Rights Movement in nonviolent direct action and nonviolent resistance to unjust laws.

He practiced personal nonviolence. If someone hit him, he did not strike back. He taught his followers to meet violence with the power of love.

While Rosa Parks agreed to the nonviolent tactics used by Dr. King, she did not believe so strongly in the principles of nonviolence. In her autobiography, *Rosa Parks: My Story*, she wrote:

> *I was raised to be proud, and it had worked for me to stand up aggressively for myself. . . . On an individual level, nonviolence could be mistaken for cowardice. . . . However, with the entire African American population of Montgomery going the nonviolent way, I saw that the tactic could be successful. . . . To this day, I am not an absolute supporter of nonviolence in all situations.*

Make copies of the Principles of Nonviolence and tape them onto 5-by-7 index cards, one for each participant.

Begin by gathering a group of four to eight friends. Together, read the "Introduction to Nonviolence."

Distribute the cards with the Principles of

Nonviolence. Dr. King believed in nonviolence as a moral principle. Rosa Parks believed in nonviolence as a tactic that worked. Discuss the difference between these two positions. What do you think about nonviolence?

Many different actions qualify as nonviolent direct action. In Gene Sharp's book, *The Methods of Nonviolent Action*, he lists 198 methods of nonviolent protest and persuasion. A few of the methods listed are: petitions, slogans and symbols to communicate with a wider audience, picketing, boycotts, vigils, singing, and strikes. What methods of nonviolent action have you participated in? Heard about? Witnessed? Discuss.

Put your words into action! One of the methods of nonviolent action is displaying banners, posters, and other forms of communications. Some schools observe a peace week and display student posters in the hallways. Some places of worship display artwork created by their religious school classes. Choose an issue that is important to you. Design a banner or poster and find a place to display it.

Note: This activity can be adapted for use in a classroom—or around the family dinner table.

Principles of Nonviolence

These are adapted from the teaching of Dr. Martin Luther King, Jr.

1. Nonviolence resists evil and oppression.

2. Nonviolence seeks to win the friendship and understanding of the opponent—not to humiliate or defeat the opponent.

3. Nonviolence attacks the forces of evil, not the persons doing the evil.

4. Nonviolence accepts suffering without retaliating.

5. Nonviolence is based on love—and that includes loving one's opponents.

6. The person who practices nonviolence believes in the future and believes that some day justice will triumph.

Walk for Justice

The black people of Montgomery, Alabama, walked for a year instead of riding segregated buses. They showed their commitment to justice. You, too, can walk for justice!

Directions

Begin by deciding who will walk, why you will walk, when and where you will walk, and how you will celebrate your success!

Who will walk?

Who do you know that shares your commitment to civil rights and justice for all? Maybe your classmates at school would like to walk with you. Maybe a group such as the Girl Scouts or 4-H would sponsor a walk, or another organization, church, synagogue, or mosque in your community.

Why will you walk?

You can walk to raise money for one of the organizations that is working for justice today. Make up a pledge sheet and make copies for walkers. Collect pledges before the big day.

Here's an example of a pledge sheet.

**Pledge Sheet
Walk for Justice**

I, Jane Mason, will be walking for justice on Tuesday, June 21. With 11 other young people from my church, I will walk for 2 miles. All the money that we collect will be donated to the Southern Poverty Law Center to support their Teaching Tolerance program. Will you help by donating $1 or more for each mile that I march?

Pledged by	Amount per mile	Total amount
_____	_____	_____
_____	_____	_____
_____	_____	_____
_____	_____	_____
_____	_____	_____
_____	_____	_____
_____	_____	_____

Thank you!

Here are some good organizations to support.

Highlander Research and Education Center works with social activists, educators, and grassroots leaders (primarily from the South and Appalachia) who are engaged in efforts that promote social justice. Rosa Parks is one of their alumni!

1959 Highlander Way
New Market, TN 37820
Telephone (423) 933-3443
Fax (423) 933-3424
E-mail   hrec@igc.apc.org

Mexican American Legal Defense and Educational Fund works through litigation, advocacy, law school and communications scholarships, and community education and activation to secure the civil rights of Latinos living in the United States.

634 South Spring Street
11th Floor
Los Angeles, CA 90014
Telephone (213) 629-2512
Fax (213) 629-8016

National Association for the Advancement of Colored People (NAACP) has been a pioneer and leader in the civil rights struggle since its founding in 1909.

4805 Mount Hope Drive
Baltimore, MD 21215
Telephone (410) 358-8900
Fax (410) 486-9255

Southern Christian Leadership Conference (SCLC), founded in 1957 by Dr. Martin Luther King, Jr., Dr. Joseph E. Lowery, and others, is an interfaith advocacy organization dedicated to using the principles of nonviolence as a strategy for bringing about social, economic, and political justice.

> 334 Auburn Ave, N.E.
> Atlanta, GA 30303
> Telephone (404) 522-1420
> Fax (404) 659-7390

Southern Poverty Law Center (SPLC) works through litigation and educational programs to protect and advance the legal rights of poor people and minorities. SPLC sponsors Teaching Tolerance, a project that supplies educators at all levels with free publications and videos that provide ideas, resources, and techniques for teaching tolerance in a diverse society.

> Box 548
> 400 Washington Avenue
> Montgomery, AL 36104
> Telephone (334) 264-0286
> Fax (334) 264-0629
> Web site   www.splcenter.org/

When and where?

Pick a day and a destination. Do you want to march around a lake? To a school? To your city hall? Do you want to do something as you march, like pick up trash along a trail? Do you want to carry signs? Or wear special T-shirts? You could draw a pattern for a rainbow design, representing all the colors of people in the world, and then paint the design on inexpensive cotton T-shirts for marchers.

How will you celebrate your success?

You could rent a movie about the Civil Rights Movement, such as *Mississippi Burning*, and watch it together at the end of your walk. (See Additional Resources at the end of the book for more movie suggestions.) Be sure to count the pledges you collect and tell everyone who walked and everyone who pledged about your success. Celebrate with popcorn or pizza or ice cream sundaes all around.

Alternative Holidays

During the bus boycott, the merchants of downtown Montgomery suffered losses because their black customers stayed away. They brought pressure on civic leaders to try to find a solution so that they would not lose more business. Consumers often use dollar power to influence business policies and decisions. They can use dollar power negatively by boycotting businesses. They can also use dollar power positively, by buying from companies or organizations whose practices they wish to support.

Directions

You can organize friends and family to support companies and organizations that help poor people around the world. You can contact a fair trade or alternative trade organization and locate a store near you. You can get a catalog and collect orders from friends and family. Here are some addresses to get started.

SERRV International is a nonprofit program that promotes the social and economic progress of people in developing regions of the world by purchasing and marketing their crafts in a just and direct manner. When you buy products from SERRV International, your purchase brings dignity and needed income to a developing world artisan. Contact SERRV for more information or a free catalog.

Telephone (800) 723-3712

E-mail   info@serrv.org

The Fair Trade Federation (FTF) is an association of fair trade wholesalers, retailers, and producers whose members are committed to providing fair wages and good employment opportunities to economically disadvantaged artisans and farmers worldwide. FTF directly links low-income producers with consumer markets and educates consumers about the importance of purchasing fairly traded products that support living wages and safe and healthy conditions for workers in the Third World. They can provide you with information or lists of retailers.

Web site   www.fairtradefederation.com/

Ten Thousand Villages is a nonprofit alternative trading organization that provides vital, fair income to Third World people by selling their handicrafts and telling their stories in North America. Ten Thousand Villages works with artisans who would otherwise be unemployed or underemployed. Ten Thousand Villages is a program of Mennonite Central Committee (MCC), the service, relief, and development agency of Mennonite and Brethren in Christ churches in North America.

704 Main Street
P.O. Box 500
Akron, PA 17501-0500
Telephone (717) 859-8100
Fax (717) 859-2622
E-mail   inquiry@villages.ca

3

Nonviolent Resistance

Student Sit-Ins, 1960

Nonviolent Resistance

Introduction

Black college students across the South felt the oppressive weight of segregation. Many were better educated than white people who drove segregated buses or waited on tables in segregated restaurants. They were less patient than their elders who had suffered decades of discrimination. They had seen the success of nonviolent action in Montgomery. They were ready to take action themselves.

Woolworth's Lunch Counter

Monday, February 1, 1960, Greensboro, North Carolina. Four black students from North Carolina A & T College entered Woolworth's Department Store. They sat down at the lunch counter. The waitress refused to serve them. Like every restaurant in Greensboro, Woolworth's lunch counter was segregated. Unlike Montgomery's buses, the lunch counter did not have separate seating for black people. It had *no* seating for black people. Woolworth's five-and-dime store sold goods to black and white people, but its lunch counter served only white people.

The four young men sat there all afternoon. They were never served. When they finally left, they promised to be back at ten o'clock the next morning to continue their sit-down protest against segregation.

That night telephone lines buzzed. More students wanted to join them. Even some white students from Greensboro College wanted to sit in. Student leaders organized the new recruits. By Tuesday morning, 19 more students joined the first 4. By Wednesday, 85 students were taking turns sitting in. They arranged their lunch counter sit-in shifts so that they could also attend classes.

The white managers of the Greensboro Woolworth's did not know how to respond. At first, they did not have the young people arrested. By the end of the first week, the sit-in had attracted hundreds of eager students. They began sitting in at Kress, another big downtown store.

A minister who supported the Greensboro students called civil rights leader Jim Lawson in Nashville, Tennessee. Lawson and some Nashville students had been planning and preparing a similar action. Adult civil rights leaders had helped to train Nashville students in the theory and practice of nonviolent protest. Now the Nashville students began a sympathy sit-in that quickly escalated into a mass movement.

The Greensboro students themselves contacted other civil rights leaders. Quickly recognizing the importance of the new sit-in movement, Reverend King told them that they were ready to take "honored places in the worldwide struggle for freedom." He urged the students to "fill up the jails."

Greensboro was not the first sit-in protest. At least 16 other cities had been sites of sit-in protests during the previous three years. But for some reason, the sit-in at Woolworth's captured the imagination of young people across the South and across the nation. Similar protests began in other cities in North Carolina, and in South Carolina, too.

Angry white crowds surrounded the sit-in protesters. Some attacked the students. They poured ketchup over the students' heads. They burned the students with lighted cigarettes.

At first, police stood by and watched. Then they arrested the polite, well-dressed young students. They did not arrest the white tormen-

Fred Blackwell, AP/Wide World Photos

Angry young white people poured food on sit-in protesters, knocked them off lunch counter stools, and kicked and beat them. This photo is from a lunch counter in Jackson, Mississippi, in 1963.

tors. Black college students, the pride and joy of their law-abiding families, were hauled off to jails across the South.

In Nashville, Tennessee, Diane Nash was a college student from Chicago. She took the protest one step further. In court, a judge pronounced the protesters guilty and imposed fines. Nash said she would not pay.

Nash spoke politely, representing a group of 14 protesters. She told the judge, "If we pay these fines we would be contributing to and supporting the injustice and immoral practices that have been performed in the arrest and conviction of the defendants."

Police led Nash and the others away to jail. Another 60 protesters decided to stand with them. They also refused to pay fines and remained in jail. Inspired by their example, more students joined in the protest.

Young Leaders Diane Nash and James Bevel

Diane Nash grew up in a middle-class Catholic home in Chicago. She was light-skinned enough to pass for white, had she chosen to do so. (Sometimes very light-skinned African Americans passed for white, living their lives as white people and leaving behind their African American heritage.)

When she was 15 years old, Nash saw an advertisement for a charm school for teenagers. She decided she wanted to go. She wanted to learn more about makeup and posture and manners and all the other subjects that a charm school might teach. Nash called the school to register for a class. "No," they told her. "We don't take any colored students."

A few years later, Nash moved to Nashville, Tennessee, to go to college. Attending the Tennessee State Fair with a friend, she saw for the first time the ugly signs marking "White Only" and "Colored" restrooms. Shopping in downtown Nashville, she ran into more ugliness. There, too, large signs marked segregated restrooms and restaurants. Each encounter with discrimination both hurt and angered Nash.

Back in Chicago, Nash and her friends had enjoyed shopping in downtown department stores. After shopping, they ate lunch in the stores. In Chicago and throughout much of the North, neighborhoods were segregated by custom and not by law. While some northern restaurants were reluctant to serve black people, they used super-slow service or excuses

In Chicago and throughout much of the North, neighborhoods were segregated by custom and not by law.

like "the kitchen just closed" instead of posting signs on the doors. Somehow, the laws and signs of Nashville made segregation more obvious and more hateful.

Nash had begun nonviolence training and preparation for sit-ins even before the Greensboro sit-ins began. She was determined to do her part in the struggle for justice.

As Nash sat quietly in her college class before a demonstration, she barely heard the professor talking. She was scared of being beaten, scared of jail. She watched the clock as the hands moved slowly, marking the passage of time until the next demonstration.

When the time came, Nash put away her books, combed her beautiful black hair, and marched off. She went first to the lunch counter and then to jail. Although she was terrified, she acted bravely. She became the head of Nashville's central committee for sit-ins.

Diane Nash married James Bevel, a fellow student and civil rights activist. Bevel was born the 13th of 17 children in a family in Itta Bena, Mississippi. His parents separated when Bevel was 10 years old. After high school, he enlisted in the Navy. Onboard ship, he had a lot of time to read. He became convinced that killing was absolutely wrong. He believed that killing another human being went against the teachings of Christianity. He was so certain that he convinced the Navy to discharge him because serving in the military violated his conscience.

Back in Mississippi, Bevel worked as a bricklayer and as a musician. He entered college in January 1957 at the age of 20 to study for the ministry. Like many other students who were going to be ministers, he supported himself by preaching at a small church on weekends. As he continued his study of Christian nonviolence, he was led inevitably into the growing Civil Rights Movement. On February 13, 1960, Bevel joined more than a hundred other young people sitting in at Nashville department stores.

Nash and Bevel met during their work for the movement. They fell in love and married, both remaining deeply involved in the Civil Rights Movement. In the spring of 1962 Nash was pregnant with their first child. She stood before a judge in Jackson, Mississippi. She was accused of breaking the law by leading high

On February 13, 1960, Bevel joined more than a hundred other young people sitting in at Nashville department stores.

The sit-in protesters used nonviolent resistance to defy the practice of segregating lunch counters.

school students to protest against segregation. Nash told the judge that it did not matter if her child was born in jail. She said that any black child born in Mississippi was already in prison.

Nash dropped out of college to become a brave, proud leader in the Civil Rights Movement that would change America.

Like Nash, Bevel quickly became a leader in the young Civil Rights Movement. His voice was also one of the first raised in protest against the Vietnam War.

Nonviolent Resistance

The student protesters were practicing nonviolent resistance and civil disobedience. Many based their commitment to nonviolence on Christian principles. They quoted the scripture passages in which Jesus told his followers to love their enemies and to turn the other cheek when attacked.

Nonviolent resistance to evil also has non-Christian roots. Henry David Thoreau (1817–1862), an American philosopher, wrote about nonviolence and civil disobedience. (Civil disobedience is part of nonviolent resistance.

Civil disobedience means refusing to obey unjust laws, and accepting even jail as a consequence of that refusal.) Thoreau refused to pay taxes, saying that he could not, in good conscience, help to pay for an unjust war. He was jailed for refusing to pay taxes to support the United States war against Mexico (the Mexican War) in 1845.

In India, Gandhi used nonviolent resistance to win independence for his country. Gandhi and his followers protested British rule of India. By the thousands, Gandhi's followers accepted violence and jail instead of British rule. Eventually their nonviolent resistance proved more powerful than British military force. Thoreau's protest was an individual act of protest. Gandhi successfully used nonviolent resistance as the base for a mass movement.

The sit-in protesters used nonviolent resistance to defy the practice of segregating lunch counters. They showed a commitment to nonviolence in their response to angry white people who hit them, poured ketchup over their heads, and called them offensive names.

They were also practicing civil disobedience. They opposed not only racist custom and

Many young people participated in the Civil Rights Movement. They marched, sat in at lunch counters, demonstrated, and helped to educate others.

. . . sit-ins were followed by wade-ins at public beaches and even by pray-ins at segregated churches.

perhaps the future of the world. As the country watched the brave young people, others were inspired to join them, and the movement grew.

One of the groups was the Congress of Racial Equality (CORE). Its Rules for Action included a commitment to "Meet the anger of any individual or group in the spirit of goodwill and creative reconciliation; submit to assault and do not retaliate in kind either by act or word."

Participants shared their own reasons for believing that nonviolence was the right approach. They talked about who was willing to risk jail. Some were comfortable only with actions that did not seem to carry that risk. Of course, sometimes people who were not planning to risk arrest found themselves in handcuffs anyway.

Before going into a demonstration, the committed young people practiced on each other. They took turns playing the part of white hecklers and peaceful demonstrators. They talked about what to expect in the demonstration and after arrest. They prayed together and sang together, building bonds that made their united voices and actions strong enough to topple a centuries-old system of segregation.

racist individuals, but also the laws of segregation. With Nash, they shared a commitment to disobeying these unjust laws. The first wave of lunch counter sit-ins was followed by more sit-ins. Later, the sit-ins were followed by wade-ins at public beaches and even by pray-ins at segregated churches.

As the young protesters of the Civil Rights Movement experienced jail for the first time, their resolve strengthened. More than ever, they believed themselves part of a large movement that would change the face of the country, and

Lunch Counter Play

What Is This World Coming To?

This play re-creates the drama of a lunch counter sit-in in the early 1960s in the segregated South. You will be able to see, hear, and feel what happened in the sit-in.

Because this play involves difficult emotional issues of racism and violence, it should be carefully discussed as it is rehearsed. Actors need to think about what they are doing and why. They also need to be careful that no one is injured in the restaurant scene.

Characters

Narrator

Waitress

2 police officers

3 white hecklers

3 or 4 demonstrators, dressed in suits or
    good dresses

Because this is a play with a variable number of actors, you will need to decide which demonstrators and hecklers say what lines.

Props

6 chairs or stools

1 table

Salt and pepper shakers

Plastic ketchup bottle

Box of napkins

Crepe paper

Cloth for wiping table

Setting

Lunch counter in a southern state, 1960

Arrange six stools or chairs and a table to show a lunch counter, with salt and pepper shakers and a plastic ketchup bottle and box of napkins on the table. The table is at the far right side of the stage.

Unravel the crepe paper down the middle of the room, to suggest two different places—inside at the lunch counter and outside on the street. (Murals could be posted on the back walls of the stage to further illustrate that one place is in the street and the other inside the building.)

As the play opens, the waitress is wiping off the table. Outside in the street, the demonstrators are holding hands in a circle, heads bowed and eyes closed.

NARRATOR

Our play is set in a southern state in 1962. The Civil Rights Movement has begun to challenge old laws and traditions that forcibly separate black and white people. Among the leaders of the movement are young people, who bravely put their bodies on the line in the struggle for justice.

DEMONSTRATOR

Dear God, give us strength to challenge this unjust law. Give us peaceful, loving hearts. Help us to love those who want to be our enemies. Guide us in your way of peace and justice.

OTHER DEMONSTRATORS

Amen.

DEMONSTRATOR

Remember, no matter what they do, we are going to stay nonviolent.

DEMONSTRATOR

Are we all agreed that we go to jail if it comes to that?

OTHER DEMONSTRATORS

(speaking together)

Yes. Yes, that's right. I'm ready.

DEMONSTRATOR

Then let's go in.

(The four young people enter and sit down at the lunch counter. The waitress backs away as far as she can. She turns her back and looks over her shoulder, as if hoping they will disappear.)

DEMONSTRATOR

Excuse me, ma'am, I'd like to order.

DEMONSTRATOR

Could you bring me a cup of coffee, please?

WAITRESS

You know you all aren't supposed to be here.

The Civil Rights Movement for Kids, © 2000. Published by Chicago Review Press, Inc. 800-888-4741.

DEMONSTRATOR

We would just like to have a little something to eat.

WAITRESS

We don't serve Negroes here.

DEMONSTRATOR

Could I see a menu, please?

WAITRESS

Now, you all just get out. Just leave. I don't want any trouble.

DEMONSTRATOR

I don't want any trouble either. I am a person, just like you. I'd like a cup of coffee, please.

WAITRESS

Negroes are not allowed here. This lunch counter is only for whites. You have to leave.

NARRATOR

The waitress is a little person, caught in the middle of a big struggle. Whatever she person-ally thinks or feels, she is bound by the rules of the place where she works. And she has grown up in a segregated country. She can't quite believe that these young people are chal-lenging the way that things have always been.

(The HECKLERS enter from the left side of the stage. They stand at the middle line, as if look-ing in through a window. They whisper to one another. Then one of the DEMONSTRATORS looks back over her/his shoulder and their eyes meet. The HECKLERS enter the restaurant.)

HECKLER

Hey, nigger, don't you know this is a white lunch counter?

HECKLER

Yeah, nigger, get your black behind out of here!

DEMONSTRATOR

I would just like to have a cup of coffee.

HECKLER

Oh, yeah? Well, you don't drink coffee here. You get on back to your own side of town.

The Civil Rights Movement for Kids, © 2000. Published by Chicago Review Press, Inc. 800-888-4741.

(HECKLER *shoves* DEMONSTRATOR. *This is a staged shove, so the* DEMONSTRATOR *should act like he or she has been shoved hard.*)

HECKLER

Get on out of here, before you find some real trouble.

(HECKLER *pretends to punch* DEMONSTRATOR *in the head. Remember that these are staged or pretend punches, not real punches. Practice these so the* DEMONSTRATOR *doesn't get hurt.*)

HECKLER

Maybe you want some ketchup to go with your coffee?

(HECKLER *picks up ketchup bottle and squirts ketchup on head and back of* DEMONSTRATOR. *Ketchup squirts on countertop as well.*)

WAITRESS

Now, come on, you all. I don't want any trouble here.

HECKLER

Seems like these niggers and nigger-lovers want trouble though.

(HECKLERS *harass all the* DEMONSTRATORS.)

WAITRESS

Come on, you all. Please don't make trouble at my lunch counter. I'll have to call the police.

HECKLER

You just do that. And while you do, we'll have a little fun with these commie agitators.

The Civil Rights Movement for Kids, © 2000. Published by Chicago Review Press, Inc. 800-888-4741.

(WAITRESS goes to telephone and calls police. HECKLERS begin to pull DEMONSTRATOR off chair, kicking and punching him/her to the ground, while yelling insults. The DEMONSTRATORS say nothing. They sit quietly at the lunch counter until thrown on the floor.)

WAITRESS

(to HECKLER)

Stop! You're hurting him! You don't need to do that!

(A police siren sounds outside. Two police officers enter. They look around at the scene in the restaurant.)

OFFICER

(speaking to waitress)
Looks like you have quite a crowd here, ma'am.

WAITRESS

(in tears)

I don't know what to do. They won't leave.

(pointing to DEMONSTRATORS, at least two of whom are now on the ground.)

And they won't leave them alone.

(pointing to HECKLERS)

OFFICER

Well, I think we can handle it from here.

(speaking to HECKLERS)

You fellows run along.

DEMONSTRATOR

(getting up from the floor, his head and mouth bleeding)

I just want to order a cup of coffee.

WAITRESS

And I told you I can't serve Negroes here. Oh, Lord, what have they done to you?

OFFICER

We'll handle this.

(speaking to DEMONSTRATOR)

The Civil Rights Movement for Kids, © 2000. Published by Chicago Review Press, Inc. 800-888-4741.

You are under arrest for trespassing.

OFFICER

You are all under arrest for trespassing and disturbing the peace.

(OFFICERS handcuff DEMONSTRATORS to one another and take them out the door. Outside, the HECKLERS yell at the DEMONSTRATORS as they are led away by the police. The HECKLERS follow the police and DEMONSTRATORS offstage.)

WAITRESS

(in tears)

I don't know what this world is coming to. I just don't know.

NARRATOR

We are now what her world was coming to. The laws of the United States forbid racial segregation. No restaurants can be segregated. No hotels can be segregated. Buses, trains, and airplanes must serve people of all races equally. Discrimination in employment is forbidden.

We are now what her world was coming to. In northern and southern cities, black children go to mostly-black schools and live in mostly-black neighborhoods. Black family income is still lower than white family income. And race hatred is still alive.

We are now what her world was coming to. How will we reshape our world for the future?

(All actors return to stage, join hands, and bow.)

The Civil Rights Movement for Kids, © 2000. Published by Chicago Review Press, Inc. 800-888-4741.

Freedom School

In a Freedom School you can focus on issues that are important to you and your fellow students.

The Civil Rights Movement ran summer-long Freedom Schools. Lessons focused on the values, desires, and daily lives of the students. Methods included reading, writing, role-playing, poetry, and giving speeches.

Black students in the southern United States during the 1960s suffered from poor and repressive schooling. The whole system of education tried to keep them down. White people believed that black people who were educated would become "uppity" and would not stay in "their place."

"With some people who were at the very beginning level in terms of trying to read and write, we would have things such as just regular ABCs," one Freedom School teacher recalled later. "And we also incorporated dealing with numbers. . . . We would have sections of the constitution retyped where it was in big letters, big words where people could see it, and we could begin to read and teach people to read from those. . . . In some cases we would have articles that had come out in various papers . . . and we would have people go through the process of attempting to read."

You can run your own day-long or week-long Freedom School, where students focus on their values, desires, and lives. For this project, you will need at least a dozen people. One or more leaders/teachers can help to find information resources. You can locate your Freedom School in a home, community center, or church basement.

You could also make part of your regular school a Freedom School. One class day or one class period every day for a week (or more) could be designated as Freedom School. Teachers can help to find resources and to structure learning activities. Every community and school will have its own issues.

Here are some questions and activities to help you get started with your Freedom School.

Questions

1. The *culture* of a group includes its shared beliefs and values, its manners and customs.

Each person grows up as part of a culture. What is the name of your culture? Is your culture a majority or minority in your community?

2. What is another culture that you would like to learn about? What three things would you like to learn?

3. What is one way that race makes a difference in your life?

4. How does race matter in your community?

Activities

Read and discuss

- *Black Like Me* by John Howard Griffin
- Poetry of Langston Hughes, including "What Happens to a Dream Deferred"
- Maya Angelou's poetry or memoirs, such as *I Know Why the Caged Bird Sings*

Watch and discuss

- *Amistad*
- *Sounder*
- *Roots*
- *I Know Why the Caged Bird Sings*
- Other videos

Role play

- Conversation between heckler and demonstrator in Woolworth's lunch counter sit-in
- Conversation between jailer and protester, exploring reasons that the individual is willing to sit in jail
- Conversation between student and grandparent about race

More Information on Freedom Schools

One of the groups organizing the 1960s Freedom Schools noted that their most important goal was "to implant habits of free thinking and ideas of how a free society works."

Jimmy Garrett, another activist, wrote *Freedom Schools*. These schools were important beyond the South, and for young white people as well as young black people.

My idea of a Freedom School is an area, atmosphere, a situation—any place where young people, whether black or white, rich or poor, come to deal with real questions as they relate to their lives. The aim of this part of the Freedom School would be to let young people challenge not only the authority which stifles them, but also to challenge themselves, to bring about basic changes within the system so that the stifling ends.

One curriculum for Freedom Schools posed these questions:

1. What does the majority culture have that we want?
2. What does the majority culture have that we don't want?
3. What do we have that we want to keep?
4. What do we have that we don't want to keep?

Freedom Schools talked about very concrete needs of their students and communities—about food, clothing, shelter, work and working conditions, voting, and participation in the life of the community.

"If Not Us, Then Who?"

Freedom Riders, 1961

"If Not Us, Then Who?"

Introduction

Some of the people inspired by the college student sit-ins decided to take action against continuing segregation in public transportation. They knew that southern states insisted on separate seating, restrooms, restaurants, and waiting rooms for blacks and whites. They also knew that more than a dozen years earlier, the Supreme Court had ruled this segregation illegal. They decided to take the radical action of following the law laid down by the Supreme Court.

Beginning the Freedom Rides

Thirteen men and women gathered in Washington, D.C., in the spring of 1961. They came to begin training as Freedom Riders. Their ages ranged from 21 to 60. Among them were students, a professor, a folk singer, a preacher, and a writer. Some were black and some were white. Some of the group belonged to CORE. Two belonged to the Student Nonviolent Coordinating Committee (SNCC).

CORE was founded in 1942 and used sit-ins and physical protests to challenge segregation in Chicago at that time. In 1947 CORE demonstrators rode buses through Virginia and North Carolina to challenge segregation on interstate transportation. Now they would join in the Freedom Rides of 1961.

SNCC grew out of the student sit-in movement in Nashville, Tennessee, and other southern cities. SNCC represented the younger generation of the Civil Rights Movement. They were more radical than their elders. SNCC members committed their entire lives to the Civil Rights Movement. They gave up college, jobs, security, even families. They put their bodies on the line, risking beatings and death.

SNCC used nonviolent protest to appeal to people's hearts. SNCC's methods included demonstrations or direct action and arrests. The young people of SNCC were impatient. They wanted change now.

Their elders in the Civil Rights Movement often disagreed with the tactics of SNCC and the younger generation. More experienced leaders believed that slower movement was effective. The NAACP, for example, focused on changing laws and emphasized lawsuits and legal action to end segregation.

Thirteen men and women gathered in Washington, D.C., in the spring of 1961. They came to begin training as Freedom Riders. Their ages ranged from 21 to 60.

Older leaders also feared the risks that young people took. They did not want to see their sons and daughters beaten, jailed, or even killed. They wanted to protect the younger generation.

Leaders of the Student Nonviolent Coordinating Committee

The leaders of the new organization came from many different places. Diane Nash and James Bevel were leaders introduced in Chapter 3, "Nonviolent Resistance: Student Sit-Ins, 1960." John Lewis was another important leader during the Freedom Rides.

John Lewis grew up on a small farm in Alabama. His father and mother worked long and hard hours working in farm fields alongside their children. Many of Lewis's nine brothers and sisters liked working in the fields better than going to school. Young Lewis liked school better. Sometimes when the children were kept home from school to work in the fields, Lewis would sneak away from the farm to go to school.

The one kind of farm work that young John Lewis liked was taking care of chickens. He took charge of the family's flock. From an early age, Lewis felt called to be a minister. Soon he decided that the chickens were his congregation. He preached to the chickens, telling them to lead good lives and stop quarreling with one

Bus stops were completely segregated—from waiting rooms to bathrooms to dining rooms. Here's an outhouse on the road between Louisville, Kentucky, and Nashville, Tennessee, from 1943.

another. When a chicken died, Lewis gave it a proper burial and preached a eulogy.

As a youngster, Lewis was fascinated by the forbidden topics of racism and segregation. He sneaked around to listen to adult conversations, hiding under chairs until discovered and removed.

Lewis preached his first real sermon at the age of 16 at the Macedonia Baptist Church. At about the same time, he listened to Dr. Martin Luther King, Jr. preach on the radio. Lewis was excited at the connections that Dr. King drew between Christian commitment and changing the world.

When he entered the university, Lewis encountered early civil rights organizing efforts. Joining the nonviolence training sessions, he quickly became a leader in SNCC.

Leadership was not glamorous. Leading SNCC members meant leading others and himself into danger. Lewis did not hesitate. When people counseled caution, he responded: "If not us, then who? If not now, then when? Will there be a better day for it tomorrow or next year? Will it be less dangerous then? Will someone else's children have to risk their lives instead of us risking ours?" As a SNCC leader, Lewis endured arrests, jail, beatings, and even a fractured skull.

At the age of 23, he spoke for SNCC and the younger generation at the 1963 March on Washington. (See Chapter 6, "I Have a Dream: March on Washington, 1963.") Standing shoulder to shoulder with Dr. King and other leaders, John Lewis proclaimed: "We want our freedom and we want it now!"

Twenty-three years later, Lewis returned to Washington as a congressman from Georgia. The boy who preached to the chickens had grown to a man whose wisdom and courage could guide the nation.

An Unknown Leader

Unlike Diane Nash, James Bevel, and John Lewis, Ella Baker was in her late 50s at the time of the Freedom Rides. She was born in 1903 in Virginia and grew up in North Carolina. Her parents insisted that all three Baker children get good educations. Ella Baker graduated from Shaw University in 1927. Moving to New York City, she worked as a waitress, factory worker, and reporter. She helped to begin cooperatives during the Great Depression and soon began working for the NAACP. In *cooperatives* people pooled their money to buy food in large quantities. In this way, they got lower prices and more food for their money.

As a worker for the NAACP, Baker returned to the South to do grassroots organizing. She wanted to help poor people, and she believed in strong people, not just strong leaders. During the 1960s, she left the NAACP and helped to organize the SCLC, serving as its executive director. Because she was a woman, Baker's name is not famous. In the early days of the movement, all the glory went to the men.

Years later, she recalled: "The personality that had to be played up was Dr. King. The other organizations . . . the executive director was the spokesman. But they couldn't tolerate having an old lady, even a lady, and an old lady at that. It was too much for the masculine and ministerial ego to have permitted that."

Ella Baker did not care who got the glory. She was happy to work hard and get results, always trying hard to spread power among many people. Baker encouraged young people to take leader-

ship roles and to build their own organization. She advised the young people who founded SNCC and served as a bridge between them and their elders in other civil rights organizations.

During the Freedom Summer of 1964 (see Chapter 5, "Standing Up for Freedom: From Birmingham to Selma, 1963–1965), Baker also advised the Mississippi Freedom Democratic Party.

On the Bus

The Freedom Riders rode Greyhound and Trailways buses some 1,500 miles from Washington, D.C., all the way to New Orleans. Some white members of the group rode in the back of the

> ### The Boynton Decision
>
> The U.S. Supreme Court decided the case of Boynton versus Virginia in December 1960. Segregation in interstate buses had already been ruled illegal decades earlier. Now the Boynton decision said that segregation was illegal in all waiting rooms and restaurants serving interstate bus passengers.

Baker encouraged young people to take leadership roles and to build their own organization.

On the morning of
May 6, the violence
began.

Though Greyhound was a national bus company, it observed southern segregation laws in southern states as evidenced by this waiting room sign in Rome, Georgia, 1943.

bus. Some black members of the group rode in the front. Some black and white Freedom Riders sat together. They ignored "White" and "Colored" signs on restrooms and waiting rooms.

On May 4, 1961, the first day of their 13-day journey, everything went well. Some people glared angrily at the mixed-race group, but no one bothered them. On May 5, they were turned away from the waiting room in one town. On the morning of May 6, the violence began.

The bus stopped at the Greyhound terminal in Rock Hill, South Carolina. John Lewis, a 21-year-old SNCC student, walked toward the "white" waiting room. Two young white men stepped in front of him. They told him to go to the "colored" entrance. Lewis refused. "I have a right to go in here on grounds of the Supreme Court decision in the Boynton case," he said. The white men attacked.

First they knocked Lewis to the ground. Then they beat down Albert Bigelow, a Harvard-educated former Navy captain, as Bigelow stepped between Lewis and his attackers. After that, Genevieve Hughes, a third Freedom Rider, was beaten to the ground. Local police moved in. The police chief offered to press assault charges against the young white hoodlums. The Freedom Riders refused. Their code of nonviolence and love did not allow them to ask for the arrest of their attackers.

During the next week, personal emergencies called away Lewis and another Freedom Rider. Other Freedom Riders joined the group. On May 13 the group arrived in Atlanta. Dr. Martin Luther King, Jr. celebrated the Freedom Riders' completion of their first 700 miles.

Into the Deep South

Now they headed into the Deep South, beginning the hardest part of the journey.

At Anniston, Alabama, a mob armed with

AP/Wide World Photos

Angry white people attacked the Freedom Riders and the buses they rode.

clubs, knives, and iron pipes waited. When the Greyhound bus carrying nine Freedom Riders and five other passengers pulled into the station, the mob slashed bus tires and beat on the door and the sides of the bus. They screamed for the blood of the Freedom Riders.

Undercover state police agents were riding on the bus, too. They were under orders to spy on the Freedom Riders. They had no intention of protecting the Freedom Riders, whom they

When someone threw a firebomb through the broken back window, the mob barricaded the door.

considered enemies and probably communists. But they did not want to be dragged outside and beaten by a mob who did not know their identities, so they ordered the driver to keep the door closed.

The driver revved up the bus, heading out of town as fast as he could go. A long trail of cars pursued the bus. As its slashed tires went flat, the bus stopped at the side of the road. The driver ran away into the fields.

Now the mob surrounded the bus, smashing windows. When someone threw a firebomb through the broken back window, the mob barricaded the door. If they could not beat the Freedom Riders, they would burn them to death inside the bus.

A desperate state police officer inside the bus pulled his gun and forced the mob to open the door. Choking on smoke, he and the passengers stumbled out. More state troopers arrived, firing their guns in the air. They drove the mob away from the bruised and bleeding Freedom Riders. The police then took the Freedom Riders to the Anniston hospital.

Meanwhile, the Trailways bus arrived in Anniston. White men got on the bus and beat these Freedom Riders until they were bloody. Then they threw the Freedom Riders into the backseats and allowed the bus to continue on its way.

In Birmingham the Ku Klux Klan prepared to meet the buses. Birmingham police cooperated with the Klan. Like the Klan, they hated the civil rights workers and considered them enemies. When the Trailways bus arrived at the station, the white men who had beaten the Freedom Riders got off first and disappeared into the crowd. Then the bloody Freedom Riders stepped off the bus.

Enraged Klansmen attacked. In blind fury, they beat even uninvolved bystanders. Seven bystanders were beaten so badly that they ended up in the hospital. The Klansmen clubbed a white reporter and smashed his camera.

Miraculously, all the Freedom Riders escaped alive. They found their way to the home of black minister Fred Shuttlesworth. There they heard by telephone from the Greyhound Freedom Riders in Anniston. Hospital officials in Anniston said their presence endangered other patients. The Anniston hospital was forcing the Freedom Riders out, where the mob was waiting for them.

Birmingham ministers organized a car caravan. Together, they rescued the wounded from Anniston. Others took the badly injured Trailways riders to Birmingham hospitals.

Because so many reporters were attacked by the angry white mobs, the Freedom Riders' story was well reported. The Freedom Riders made headlines across the country and around the world. Even the *Birmingham News* printed a front-page editorial asking "Where were the police?"

The next day, angry mobs remained around the bus station. Phone lines between Washington and Birmingham hummed. Reverend Fred Shuttlesworth spoke to Attorney General Robert Kennedy. Kennedy spoke to Alabama Governor John Patterson. Patterson spoke to Birmingham Police Commissioner Bull Connor.

Robert Kennedy and his brother, President John F. Kennedy, did not want to send federal marshals into Alabama to protect the riders. Neither Patterson nor Connor wanted federal forces in the state. Shuttlesworth wanted protection for the embattled Freedom Riders, no matter who provided it.

After prolonged telephone negotiations, the

"They Will Walk Together"

At a mass meeting in support of the Freedom Riders, Reverend Fred Shuttlesworth praised their courage and persistence. He said: "When white men and black men are beaten up together, the day is coming when they will walk together."

Attorney General reported to Reverend Shuttlesworth that Connor had promised protection to the Freedom Riders as far as the city limits.

The Freedom Riders thought this promise meant little. They pointed out that the attack in Anniston had come just outside the city limits. Then Greyhound said they could not take the Freedom Riders even as far as the city limits. They could not find a driver who would take the Freedom Riders anywhere. An angry Attorney General threatened to send an Air Force plane down to rescue the Freedom Riders.

At this point, all the Freedom Riders were bruised from their beatings. Some had teeth knocked out. One had 53 stitches closing wounds on his face. They were ready to find another way out of Birmingham.

Because so many reporters were attacked by the angry white mobs, the Freedom Riders' story was well reported.

Singing freedom songs, the Freedom Riders went to jail.

The Freedom Riders agreed to fly to New Orleans. Immediately, the mob moved to the airport. Bomb threats hit every flight scheduled to leave for New Orleans. Federal officials continued telephone negotiations with local officials. Eventually they succeeded in getting the Freedom Riders safely on a plane and out of Birmingham.

Continuing the Freedom Rides

The Freedom Rides did not end. Diane Nash and other student leaders in Nashville organized volunteers to go to Birmingham. The new riders picked up where their wounded comrades had been forced to stop. A new group of 10 riders left Nashville for Birmingham.

As the bus approached Birmingham, police flagged it down. They arrested two of the riders. They took all the non-Freedom Riders off the bus. Then the police taped newspapers over all the windows, and forced the Freedom Riders to remain on the bus in the Birmingham bus terminal for an hour.

Finally, the Freedom Riders were allowed to get off the bus. This time the Birmingham police held back the mob for three hours. After waiting for three hours, the police arrested the 10 riders and Reverend Fred Shuttlesworth. Singing freedom songs, the Freedom Riders went to jail.

More Freedom Riders came. More were beaten, jailed, and chased by angry white mobs. The federal and state government wanted to end the Freedom Rides, the violence, and the publicity. They could not. No one could stop the courageous Freedom Riders. No one could control the hatred of their racist persecutors.

United States Attorney General Robert Kennedy sent one of his top aides, John Siegenthaler, to Birmingham. After Siegenthaler was caught up in the violence and severely injured, Kennedy sent in federal marshals. Governor Patterson declared martial law and sent in the Alabama National Guard, blaming "outside agitators" and the federal government for the "disorder."

Eventually, Kennedy and state officials in Alabama and Mississippi reached an uneasy, and secret, compromise: as long as the state officials would keep mobs from attacking the Freedom Riders, Kennedy and the federal government would not object if the state police put all the Freedom Riders in jail. Publicly, Kennedy called for a "cooling-off period," asking that the civil rights workers stop the Freedom Rides. Privately, he urged that they focus instead on voter registration. As the summer wore on, wave after wave of Freedom Riders was jailed, and the rides ended.

After the Freedom Rides

Wherever the movement was active, young people appeared to work and demonstrate and fearlessly face danger. In 1960 they sat in at race-restricted lunch counters. In 1961 they joined Freedom Rides to challenge segregation on public transportation. Their bravery and their suffering captured the attention of the country.

The Freedom Rides were a dramatic part of the early days of the Civil Rights Movement. As the Freedom Rides ended, SNCC members gathered at the Highlander Center to debate their future strategies. Should they commit to continued direct actions, like the sit-ins and Freedom Rides, or should they turn to voter registration campaigns? In the end, they decided to do both.

During the Freedom Rides, even the older and more established civil rights organizations had moved on to direct actions challenging segregation. As the Civil Rights Movement continued, its committed workers participated simultaneously in quiet campaigns of voter education and registration and in highly visible direct actions. In 1963 their actions would focus national attention on Birmingham and Selma.

Wherever the movement was active, young people appeared to work and demonstrate and fearlessly face danger.

Write a Freedom Ride Journal

History is written not just by scholars but also by the people who live through each era. One way that ordinary people record history is by writing diaries or journals of their experiences. Can you put yourself in the place of the people affected by the Freedom Rides and imagine what they would have recorded?

The year is 1961. The place is Birmingham, Alabama. Freedom Riders are coming tomorrow.

Directions

Imagine yourself as different people in Birmingham in 1961. Tell what you see and hear each day.

The first person in your journal is Anna Johnson. She is a white teenager at the bus station. She is going to visit her grandmother in Memphis. What does she see and hear and think?

Imagine yourself as a nine-year-old boy named Jason. Jason is black. He is traveling to Birmingham on a Greyhound bus. The Freedom Riders are on the same bus. What does Jason see and hear and think?

Joe Carter is a black prisoner in the Birmingham jail. He is awaiting trial on a traffic charge. He listens to the sheriff and the deputies talking about the Freedom Riders. What does he see and hear and think?

Invent two more people for your journal. Write at least a page about the thoughts of each person. Share your journal with your family and friends.

Musical Drama

From the Back of the Bus

This musical drama re-creates the interior of a bus during the Freedom Rides of 1961. You will be able to see, hear, and feel what happened during the Freedom Ride.

Because this play involves difficult emotional issues of racism and violence, it should be carefully discussed as it is rehearsed. Actors need to think about what they are doing and why.

Characters

Bus driver (wearing a cap and/or uniform shirt)
3 passengers on the bus

Props

Cap and/or uniform for bus driver
Chairs, one for each actor
Hat and glasses for older bus passenger

Directions

Each section of dialogue has three passengers speaking. Because this is a play with a variable number of actors, you will need to decide which passengers say what lines. For example, if you have only three actors, all three will speak in each section. If you have more actors, then different actors can be Passengers 1, 2, and 3 in each section of dialogue. Passenger 1 always should look like an older man or woman, maybe with a little gray hair, glasses, and a hat. Passenger 2 should be a young man and Passenger 3 should be a young woman.

Setting

Inside a Greyhound bus heading toward Birmingham, 1961

(Arrange chairs to represent the inside of a bus. Place two chairs together on each side of a central aisle, with at least four rows of chairs. The driver sits in the front in a single chair.)

PASSENGER 1

How long is it until we get to Birmingham?

PASSENGER 2

I think we still have three hours to go.

The Civil Rights Movement for Kids, © 2000. Published by Chicago Review Press, Inc. 800-888-4741.

DRIVER

That's right, we'll get to Birmingham in three hours.

PASSENGER 3

I feel like I am at the top of a roller coaster, and now it's going downhill, getting faster every minute, about to crash.

PASSENGER 1

Three hours can go mighty fast.

(all passengers singing)

Ain't gonna let nobody turn me around,
Turn me around, turn me around,
Ain't gonna let nobody turn me around,
Gonna keep on walkin', keep on talkin',
Gonna build a brand-new world.

PASSENGER 3

What did your folks say about your coming on this Freedom Ride?

PASSENGER 2

My father didn't want me to come. My mother didn't either, but she said I should do what I thought was right.

PASSENGER 3

I didn't tell my folks. They would only worry.

PASSENGER 1

I'm glad to see you young folks on this journey. I first took this trip back in nineteen hundred and forty-seven with the Congress of Racial Equality.

(all passengers singing)

Ain't gonna let segregation turn me around,
Turn me around, turn me around,
Ain't gonna let segregation turn me around,
Gonna keep on walkin', keep on talkin',
Gonna build a brand-new world.

PASSENGER 3

Did you feel discouraged when nothing changed after your Freedom Ride in 1947?

PASSENGER 1

Well, in a way, I was disappointed. The buses stayed segregated. But some things did change.

The Civil Rights Movement for Kids,
© 2000. Published by Chicago Review
Press, Inc. 800-888-4741.

I went to jail. I came out again. After that, I wasn't so scared of jail. Some things changed inside all of us who went on that ride. We got stronger and more determined.

PASSENGER 2

And you showed the way. You started something. Now I hope we can finish it.

PASSENGER 1

Sometimes it takes a little acorn a long time to start growing. But when it does—look out, world! A mighty oak tree is growing strong.

(all passengers singing)

Ain't gonna let no jailhouse turn me around,
Turn me around, turn me around,
Ain't gonna let no jailhouse turn me around,
Gonna keep on walkin', keep on talkin',
Gonna build a brand-new world.

PASSENGER 2

I hope we get there all right. I heard there is a mob of Klansmen waiting for us.

PASSENGER 3

There probably is. The Birmingham police and even the FBI won't do anything to protect us.

PASSENGER 1

The police are never our protection. We put our trust in the power of God and the power of righteousness.

PASSENGER 3

The Supreme Court said no to segregation on interstate transportation. That's the supreme law of the land.

PASSENGER 2

The police don't uphold the law. We are the ones upholding the law.

PASSENGER 1

I'm ready to die, if that's what it comes to. At least my children will know that I did something so they will have a better life.

(all passengers singing)

The Civil Rights Movement for Kids, © 2000. Published by Chicago Review Press, Inc. 800-888-4741.

Ain't gonna let no Klansmen turn me around,
Turn me around, turn me around,
Ain't gonna let no Klansmen turn me around,
Gonna keep on walkin', keep on talkin',
Gonna build a brand-new world.

Ain't gonna let nobody turn me around,
Turn me around, turn me around,
Ain't gonna let nobody turn me around,
Gonna keep on walkin', keep on talkin',
Gonna build a brand-new world.

Standing Up for Freedom

From Birmingham to Selma, 1963–1965

Standing Up for Freedom

Connor promised to fill the jails with Negro protesters. The press and the country paid little attention.

Introduction

The seeds planted by the Freedom Rides continued to grow throughout the rest of 1961 and 1962. Despite some differences over strategy, members of the SNCC, the SCLC, and the NAACP worked on various projects across the South. Some taught in Nonviolent High, an alternative school set up in McComb, Mississippi, to serve students who had been expelled from regular high schools because of their civil rights activities. Some spread out in farming communities across Mississippi, working to organize voter education and voter registration projects. Some organized young people in Georgia. Some continued demonstrations and went to jail—in Mississippi, in Georgia, and in Alabama. Violence against black people, never punished by white authorities, continued as well.

Battle in Birmingham

In 1963 Dr. Martin Luther King, Jr. and the SCLC launched a major desegregation campaign in Birmingham, Alabama. Birmingham quickly became a highly visible battleground.

On one side were nonviolent civil rights workers. On the other side was the very violent Police Commissioner Bull Connor. April began with lunch counter sit-ins and marches on city hall. Some adults were arrested and jailed. Connor promised to fill the jails with Negro protesters. The press and the country paid little attention.

Dr. Martin Luther King, Jr. went to jail in Birmingham for nine days. From jail, he wrote an impassioned letter to white ministers who had criticized his actions and advised black people to be patient and wait.

I guess it is easy for those who have never felt the stinging darts of segregation to say "Wait." But when you have seen vicious mobs lynch your mothers and fathers at will . . . when you have seen hate-filled policemen curse, kick, brutalize, and even kill your black brothers and sisters with impunity; when you see the vast majority of your 20 million Negro brothers smothering in an air-tight cage of poverty in the midst of an affluent society . . . when you are humiliated day in and day out by nagging signs reading "white" and "colored"; when your first name becomes "nigger" and your middle name becomes "boy" (however old you are) . . . then you will understand why we find it difficult to wait.

—Letter from a Birmingham Jail

Although Dr. King's eloquent letter became famous in later years, it did not bring publicity to the struggle in Birmingham. Once out of jail, he and his fellow leaders debated what to do to make the campaign succeed. They knew that national attention was necessary.

Reverend James Bevel, a SNCC leader, had begun working on the Birmingham campaign while Dr. King was in jail. Bevel argued that the campaign should use the energy and commitment of young people, who were brave and ready to fill the jails. High school students followed college students into the movement. Grade school students wanted to demonstrate, too. Younger and younger children demanded to do their part.

Bevel said that any child old enough to belong to a church should be allowed to make

Keeping the Home Fires Burning

Dr. Martin Luther King, Jr. went to Birmingham on March 29, 1963, just two days after the birth of his fourth child, Bernice. He left Bernice and his other children in the care of their mother. Coretta Scott King was an equal partner with a different, less public role to play. She took on the hard work of raising the family in the shadow of violence and separation.

Coretta Scott learned early about hardship and danger. She was born in Alabama. She worked with her family on the farm they owned. She also worked off the farm, picking cotton to earn money for the family.

Young Scott walked six miles a day to and from school. As she walked, buses carried white children to their better schools. They stirred up dust clouds or splashed her with mud.

Scott was beautiful and gifted. She earned scholarships to high school and college. As soon as she reached college, she joined the NAACP. "From the first," she recalled, "I had been determined to get ahead, not just for myself, but to do something for my people and for all people."

After college, Scott went to the New England Conservatory of Music in Boston. She was a talented musician with a wonderful singing voice and planned to become a concert singer. She met King after a mutual friend gave her phone number to him. After she married Martin, and adding King to her name, she gave up her plan to be a singer and devoted her life, like his, to the struggle for civil rights.

On May 2, 1963, thousands of children spilled out of churches. They marched toward city hall. Most were high school students, but some were younger.

this decision. He said they could choose to demonstrate and go to jail. Even if their parents told them not to, they had a right to follow their consciences. "Against your Mama," said Bevel, "you have a right to make this witness."

Eventually, Dr. King and the other leaders agreed to lead the Birmingham young people into the campaign to end segregation. On May 2, 1963, thousands of children spilled out of churches. They marched toward city hall. Most were high school students, but some were younger. Police called in school buses to take away the children. They crammed as many as 75 young people into a jail cell intended to hold 8 adults. By that night, some 600 children were in jail. The youngest child arrested was a six-year-old girl.

The next day, more children marched. This time the fire department used high-pressure hoses. The hoses were strong enough to knock bricks loose from mortar at a distance of 100 feet—or to damage internal organs. The high-pressure hoses knocked black children off their feet. Soaking wet, gasping for air, the children rolled down the street. Still more children kept coming.

The fire hoses did not stop all the marchers. Then Police Commissioner Connor sent police dogs against the children. That night across America, families watched in horror. Television news film showed a white police officer holding a Negro teenager so that a police dog could attack him.

Young marchers remained true to their pledges of nonviolence. Crowds of people watched the march. These spectators had not promised nonviolence and had no training in it. Their anger burned as they saw children attacked by police dogs. They were outraged at the sight of children knocked down by fire hoses. Adults watching the struggle threw rocks and bricks and bottles at the police and firefighters.

That night in a Birmingham church, Dr. King spoke. The overflowing crowd included frightened parents of jailed children.

"They are suffering for what they believe, and they are suffering to make this nation a better nation," King told parents. King joked that he, too, had been bitten by a dog, when he was growing up. "I was dog-bitten for nothing," he said, "so I don't mind being bitten by a dog for standing up for my freedom!"

Now reporters from national news publishers such as *LIFE* magazine, the Associated

Press, and the *New York Times* streamed into Birmingham. Stage performer Dick Gregory and folk singer Joan Baez came, too. Dozens and then hundreds and then thousands of children and parents flowed into the streets and jails. Despite the best efforts of Connor's police, the demonstrators streamed into downtown Birmingham. Peacefully and prayerfully, they pleaded for an end to segregation. Frightened white shoppers stayed away from stores.

White businesses responded to the loss of income. They pushed the Birmingham city government to make concessions. Weeks of marching and jailing and negotiating produced agreements to desegregate downtown stores.

Victory brought more violence. Enraged racists bombed the homes and churches of civil rights leaders. Angry white people rallied after dark to the hate-filled speeches of the Ku Klux Klan. As explosions rocked the nights, people began to call the city "Bombingham."

Bill Hudson, AP/Wide World Photos

City authorities used high-powered fire hoses on demonstrators, knocking over many and even rolling them down the street with the force of the water.

Mississippi Martyr

Meanwhile in Mississippi, Medgar Evers, head of the Mississippi branch of the NAACP, began pushing for the same changes that had been so hard-won in Birmingham.

Medgar Wiley Evers had been born in 1926 in Decatur, Mississippi. He quit high school to join

Bill Hudson, AP/Wide World Photos

Police encouraged their dogs to attack demonstrators, like this teenager.

Victory brought more violence. Enraged racists bombed the homes and churches of civil rights leaders.

the United States Army in World War II. He served overseas in France. Evers had gone from a small, segregated southern town to France. He had risked his life as a soldier fighting for freedom and democracy, and had received the thanks of grateful Europeans. The war ended and he returned to segregated Mississippi. Once again, he was called "boy" and eyed with suspicion by white people wary of returning black soldiers.

Now he looked across the world for inspira-

tion. His hero was Jomo Kenyatta. Kenyatta led the African country of Kenya. Revolutionary movements for freedom struggled in Africa, as Africans fought for freedom from European colonial rulers. Evers dreamed of a revolution for black people in the South. After the war, he enrolled in Alcorn A & M College. There he met Myrlie Beasley.

Myrlie Beasley had grown up in Vicksburg, Mississippi, in the heart of the Deep South. Her parents separated when she was young. Beasley was raised by her grandmother and an aunt. Both were school teachers and strong women. Beasley prepared to follow in their footsteps.

She entered Alcorn A & M College in 1950. On her very first day on campus, she met a tall, strong football player named Medgar Evers. Evers swept her off her feet. They were married on Christmas Eve a year later. The new Mrs. Evers left college, and Medgar finished his degree. (In those days a married woman seldom pursued her own education or career.)

After college, Medgar Evers began work as an insurance salesman and in 1954 he went to work for the NAACP. Myrlie Evers shared his commitment. When he headed the Mississippi

NAACP, she became his secretary. Together, they worked to help black people register to vote. Years later, she recalled the dangers faced by black voters.

Their names would be published in the newspaper with their addresses and phone numbers, and they would be harassed by phone calls, people driving by, throwing rocks, eggs, firebombs. . . . Or the banks would call in mortgages with no notice. People got fired from their jobs immediately. Or lassoed as they were walking home, dragged into a car [and beaten]. All because they wanted to vote.

Myrlie and Medgar Evers faced even greater dangers. They taught their children to throw themselves on the floor if they heard a strange noise outside the house. "We lived with death as a constant companion 24 hours a day," she said. One night their home was firebombed. Medgar was away at a meeting. Myrlie got the garden hose and put out the flames.

Both the Everses expected that some day he would be murdered. They promised one another that they would never part in anger. They cher-ished each good-bye as if it were their last.

During the 1960s tension ran high. In 1963 Evers faced conflict with the national NAACP leadership. They did not approve of Jackson's active Civil Rights Movement. Hundreds of young people were jailed in protests. The NAACP did not agree with their tactics of civil disobedience. Medgar honored the young heroes. Secretly, he cooperated with the SCLC, which supported the young people.

He demanded that the mayor of Jackson, Mississippi, appoint an integrated committee to plan desegregation. The mayor refused.

Then the protests began. Four students and a white professor from Tougaloo College sat down at a Woolworth's lunch counter in Jackson. A white mob began by pouring mustard and ketchup all over them. Then the mob dragged demonstrators off their lunch counter stools to beat and kick them.

Suddenly, photos from Jackson made the national news. At first, the NAACP was reluctant to endorse demonstrations. Jackson's Negro children were determined to match the courage of the Birmingham children. And they did. On June 1, 1963, NAACP national leader Roy

Medgar Evers demanded that the mayor of Jackson, Mississippi, appoint an integrated committee to plan desegregation. The mayor refused.

Wilkins joined their protest. With hundreds of demonstrators and Evers, Wilkins went to jail.

All across the South, protests sprang up. Florida, North Carolina, Alabama, Georgia, Mississippi—yes, even that most segregated of southern states saw stirrings of protest. Mississippi responded with violence.

On Sunday, June 9, 1963, Annell Ponder of the SCLC joined five friends in Tennessee. They rode a Trailways bus back to Mississippi from the Highlander School. At a stop in Winona, Mississippi, Ponder walked into the "whites only" waiting room. She was immediately thrown out. When she tried to write down the license numbers of the police cars, the police arrested all six women.

Behind closed doors at the police station, the officers beat the women bloody. Word soon reached civil rights leaders that Ponder had disappeared. Lawrence Guyot, a SNCC student, drove to Winona to investigate. He, too, disappeared inside the jail. He, too, was beaten. None of the prisoners was allowed to make a phone call. No one could find them. For four days they were held inside the jail. When all seven were finally released, they were still black and blue and bloody.

Back in Tennessee, the local sheriff raided the Highlander School. He arrested 27 people for holding an interracial meeting and closed the school. Four days later the school was burned down.

Thousands of demonstrators marched in Washington, D.C. Civil rights leaders begged President John F. Kennedy and the federal government to help them.

In Jackson, Mississippi, on June 11, 1963, Medgar and Myrlie Evers embraced before he left for work. Medgar called home several times that day to tell Myrlie that he loved her. He would be home late that night, after a meeting.

That night, President John Kennedy announced that he was sending a civil rights bill to Congress. Myrlie and the children sat up to watch his speech on television. Together, they waited for Medgar to return. Just after midnight, they heard his car. And then they heard a gunshot. The children dropped to the floor, as they had been taught. Myrlie ran outside to find Medgar bleeding and dying.

Ten days later, Ku Klux Klan member Byron De La Beckwith was arrested. Jackson police felt no hostility toward the white man who had killed the black NAACP organizer. To many white Mississipians, Beckwith was a hero. The police left his cell door open and let him move freely about the police station.

Beckwith's first two trials ended in mistrials. The white juries would not convict him. They did not want to send a white man to jail for murdering Evers. Beckwith was freed in April 1964. He remained free for 30 years.

As years passed, Myrlie Evers frequently returned to Mississippi to work for a new trial for her husband's murderer. She persisted despite the unwillingness of police and attorneys to cooperate. Finally, in 1994 Byron De La Beckwith was convicted of the murder of Medgar Evers and sentenced to life in prison.

Bloody Sunday, Bloody Selma

Birmingham's children won a victory. The Civil Rights Movement won many victories. After each victory, it seemed that a new struggle lay ahead. In 1965 the struggle moved to Selma, Alabama.

On January 22, 1965, more than a hundred black teachers marched to the courthouse in Selma. The participation of black professionals in the desegregation movement energized others. Students soon followed. Sheriff Jim Clark was furious. On February 10, 1965, Clark told reporters that he had arrested the students for truancy and was marching them six miles to the Fraternal Order of Police Lodge because the jail was full. Along the way, he said with a wink, the students escaped. Marchers told another story. They had been driven out of town by deputies armed with billy clubs and cattle prods. The deputies forced the young people to keep running until some fell from exhaustion and others were left vomiting. Sheriff Clark had ridden beside the procession in his car.

A week later, the SCLC held a night march in nearby Marion. Police and state troopers attacked the marchers. Jimmy Lee Jackson, a black Vietnam veteran, tried to protect his mother as they both participated in the march. Jackson was shot. He died seven days later.

Finally, in 1994 Byron De La Beckwith was convicted of the murder of Medgar Evers and sentenced to life in prison.

To protest Jackson's death, organizers planned a march from Selma to Montgomery, the state capital. The marchers set out on Sunday, March 7. Police and state troopers attacked them at the Edmund Pettus Bridge in Selma. Across the nation, horrified people saw the attack on the evening news. They watched police mercilessly beating demonstrators. The day became known as "Bloody Sunday."

Hundreds of Americans boarded planes and buses to join the civil rights workers in Selma. Among them was a white minister from Boston, Reverend James Reeb. Led by Dr. King, they marched on the following Tuesday. Then they waited for a court order allowing them to march all the way to Montgomery.

Reverend James Reeb did not know Selma. He took a wrong turn one night and ended up near the Silver Moon Cafe. The Silver Moon Cafe was a hangout for white men, many racist and angry. They attacked Reeb and beat him bloody. Within hours, he was dead.

Jimmy Lee Jackson had been a hero. He died defending his mother. But Jimmy Lee Jackson was black. The country did not pay attention to his death. Reverend James Reeb was white and a minister. His death focused national attention on Selma.

On March 21, 1965, the marchers finally left Selma for Montgomery. This time they were protected, by order of President Lyndon Johnson. Five days later they reached Montgomery. Some 25,000 people marched into Montgomery.

Viola Liuzzo, a white woman from Detroit, was one of the 25,000. That night she drove back from Montgomery to Selma. She never made it. Along the way, she was murdered by the Ku Klux Klan.

Marching for Justice

When their children sat in Birmingham jails, parents gathered each night at the mass meetings to pray and sing. When civil rights workers went into jails, they sang and preached to one another. At each step of the march toward freedom, celebration and suffering walked hand in hand.

During the violent days of 1963, as police dogs attacked children and firebombs destroyed churches, civil rights leaders began planning a celebration. They worked tirelessly toward a great national gathering that would show the depth and breadth of support for civil rights in the United States.

Corbis/Flip Schulke

Young people played an important role in the Civil Rights Movement, participating in every march and protest.

When their children sat in Birmingham jails, parents gathered each night at the mass meetings to pray and sing.

Freedom Film Festival

Many movies celebrate the heroes and achievements of the Civil Rights Movement. You can return to the action of the 1960s by watching these films with family and friends.

This could be an activity for a Boy or Girl Scout troop, for your family, or in a school, church, synagogue, or mosque. The possibilities are limitless!

Directions

First, choose a date and place. Then select two movies for a double feature. (See the list below for ideas.)

Next, plan to serve popcorn and other goodies. Popcorn is easy to make. Dress it up with Parmesan cheese or seasoned salt. You might add a sundae bar to the festival. Just set out ice cream and a variety of toppings. Remember the whipped cream!

If a larger group is sponsoring the festival, make posters to advertise it. A little publicity gets people excited about your event.

Finally, settle back and enjoy the movies.

What to Watch

You can probably find these great videos at your local library or video rental store:

Mississippi Burning tells the true story of the murder of three young civil rights workers in Mississippi. It also shows burning churches and violent opposition to civil rights. The movie shows the FBI in a favorable light. That is not how civil rights workers remember the FBI's role.

Malcolm X traces Malcolm's life from childhood to death. It shows the poverty and racism he endured as a child. As a teenager, Malcolm became involved in crime and went to prison. There he converted to Islam. Later he moved beyond Elijah Muhammad's black separatism.

Sounder shows an African American family's struggle. They live in the rural South in the mid-twentieth century. The father is jailed for stealing food. The mother quietly and courageously keeps the family together. Her children help her to do so. The family suffers from both poverty and racism.

Roots is based on a book by Alex Haley called *Roots: The Saga of an American Family*, published in 1976. The movie traces his family roots from twentieth-century United States back to Africa. The richness of African culture shines through. The movie does not gloss over the cruelty of slavery. It shows the strength of African American families. *Roots* was broadcast as a television series in 1977. The eight-night series set records for the number of viewers. The drama inspired a surge of interest in family histories. People of all ethnic backgrounds began their own research.

A Gentleman's Agreement and *Guess Who's Coming to Dinner* are two older movies. Both show prejudice and its effects. The "gentleman's agreement" discriminates against Jews. The surprise dinner guest is Sidney Poitier. He stars as the African American fiancé of a white woman. In the movie, he comes to dinner to meet her parents.

Hoop Dreams is a documentary. It records the lives of two young African American men. They live in Chicago's inner city. Each hopes that basketball will be a ticket out of poverty. They face many obstacles. College and professional basketball systems manipulate their hopes and talents.

I Know Why the Caged Bird Sings shows part of the early life of Maya Angelou. It is based on her autobiographical memoir.

Brother Future takes a contemporary teenager on a trip in time back to the 1850s and slavery. (This is a Wonderworks production.)

And the Children Shall Lead shows black and white southern children struggling with racism in the 1960s. (This is a Wonderworks production.)

You Must Remember This explores the history of black filmmaking in the 1940s. (This is a Wonderworks production.)

Dressing to Express

You can express your creativity and your political commitments in the way that you dress. Without spending a lot of money on a new wardrobe, you can add meaningful designs to clothing that you already own.

Materials

Sturdy shirt, jacket, bib overalls, or jeans
Tailor's chalk pencil
Fabric paint
Paintbrushes, various widths
Embroidery floss
Embroidery hoop
Needle
Buttons (optional)

Directions

Begin by selecting a sturdy sweatshirt, bib overalls, or denim jeans or jacket. The fabric needs to be sturdy because you will be painting or embroidering on it.

Next, decide what part of the clothing you will use for your design. You could make a small design on one pocket of your jeans or jacket, or a larger design on the front or back of a sweatshirt or the bib of a pair of overalls.

Now decide on a simple design. You might use a peace symbol or a short slogan in a decorative border. Using the tailor's chalk pencil, sketch your design onto the clothing.

Personal Style

Many of the people involved in the Civil Rights Movement expressed themselves in the way that they dressed. As a SNCC organizer in Mississippi, Bob Moses wore bib overalls, like the farm people with whom he lived and worked. Reverend James Bevel, another SNCC organizer, sometimes wore a yarmulke (a kind of hat worn by many observant Jews) to show his admiration for the Jewish prophets of the bible. Black Muslims wore very conservative clothes—suits and ties for the men and long dresses and veils for the women. Some people, like Dr. King, dressed in formal suits and ties most of the time as an expression of dignity. Others, especially student demonstrators, favored a "uniform" of blue jeans and T-shirts, rejecting formality and business attire.

You could use fabric paint to paint your design on the clothing. Be sure to read and follow the paint directions about ironing or washing the material to "set" the paint and make it permanent.

Or you could embroider your design, using embroidery floss. Embroidering is easiest if you can fit the fabric into an embroidery hoop to hold it still and flat. (Note: This would not work for a design on a pocket, but might be possible for a design on the front of a sweatshirt.)

Today, buttons are also popular for decorating clothing. If you make a large design, such as a peace symbol on the back of a denim jacket, you might want to sew buttons on in the shape of your design. Or you might use buttons to frame a slogan that you have painted or embroidered.

6

"I Have a Dream"

March on Washington, 1963

"I Have a Dream"

Introduction

Although demonstrations and voter registration campaigns focused mainly on the South, the leaders of the Civil Rights Movement knew that only a national commitment could end segregation. They believed that the Constitution guaranteed equal rights to all, regardless of color, and that Congress should pass laws to protect those rights. One way to move the politicians into action was to show them overwhelming support for civil rights. What better place to show them than in Washington, D.C.?

As the summer of 1963 began, the dreams of a young minister and an old union organizer came together. Dr. Martin Luther King, Jr. joined A. Philip Randolph and other civil rights leaders in organizing the March on Washington for Jobs and Justice.

"The Most Dangerous Negro in America"

Like King, Asa Philip Randolph (1889–1979) was the son of a minister. His father, Reverend James William Randolph, ordered both of his sons to read books and religious magazines every day. Asa and his older brother James both graduated at the top of their classes. They attended the Cookman Institute, the first Florida high school open to African American students.

Randolph did not have enough money to go to college. He decided to move north and pursue his secret dream of becoming an actor. He arrived in Harlem in 1911, at the age of 22, and enrolled in free classes at City College. Within a short time, he switched his studies from drama to politics and economics and joined the Socialist Party. He also met his future wife and lifelong companion, Lucille Green. A widow, she had worked as a teacher, but now was a beautician with her own salon.

In 1917 Randolph and a friend established a radical magazine, *The Messenger*. Soon Randolph became deeply involved in union organizing. He focused his efforts on the Pullman Company, one of the most powerful businesses in the country. During this time, the U.S. attorney general called Randolph the "most dangerous Negro in America." Randolph organized the Brotherhood of Sleeping Car Porters. He

Dr. Martin Luther King, Jr. joined A. Philip Randolph and other civil rights leaders in organizing the March on Washington for Jobs and Justice.

A. Philip Randolph led the Brotherhood of Sleeping Car Porters and was an early leader in the Civil Rights Movement.

believed in unions to protect the rights of workers and knew that black workers needed that protection. The struggle for civil rights consumed the rest of his long life.

As a key union organizer, Randolph became a national voice for African American rights. During the 1940s and 1950s he demanded jobs and equal rights. He first proposed a March on Washington for jobs and equal rights in the 1940s. He called off the march only when President Franklin D. Roosevelt banned discrimination in government employment. President Roosevelt said defense contractors could not discriminate on the basis of race. He set up a Fair Employment Practices Committee.

In 1947 Randolph worked to end segregation in the U.S. military. He worked with younger people in a nonviolent campaign of civil disobedience. President Truman banned discrimination in the military by executive order in 1948. Then Randolph called off the civil disobedience. His action angered many younger people who wanted to continue to press for more rights.

Though he met with racism and opposition within the union movement, Randolph

Brotherhood of Sleeping Car Porters

As railroads grew, the Pullman Company became more and more powerful. Pullman sleeping cars and dining cars were placed on luxury trains of many railroads. They were still run by the Pullman Company that had manufactured them. Every Pullman conductor was white. All the Pullman porters were black. The porters worked long hours for low pay taking care of all the needs of train passengers. They staffed all the dining cars, handled luggage, and took care of sleeping cars. They received no pay for overtime. In 1920, the Pullman Company set up a puppet union to prevent workers from organizing a real union to fight for their rights.

When the American Federation of Labor (AFL) was organized in 1881, many unions excluded black workers from membership. By 1902 there were only 41,000 black workers among the 1.2 million union workers in the United States. When the Brotherhood of Sleeping Car Porters was organized in 1925, its African American members could not count on help from the AFL. The Pullman Company fired porters who worked for the union, sent spies to union meetings, and denounced the union as "red" or "Communist."

The Pullman Company also tried to bribe A. Philip Randolph. The company sent him a blank check, telling him he could write his own price if he would stop his organizing efforts. The bribe attempt backfired. Randolph made a photograph of the check and displayed it for all to see!

In 1937 the Brotherhood of Sleeping Car Porters became the first major black union to sign a contract with an employer. Without a contract, workers have few rights. A *contract* is an agreement that sets the terms of employment, including wages, overtime, sick days, and more. During the 1940s, Randolph led the union into the national union organization of the AFL-CIO. Randolph became a leader within the AFL-CIO for equal rights for all union members, regardless of the color of their skin.

Over the years, the number of railroad jobs has declined. In 1978 the Brotherhood of Sleeping Car Porters merged with the Brotherhood of Railway and Airline Clerks.

Randolph first proposed a March on Washington for jobs and equal rights in the 1940s.

... the march would pressure the federal government to act to protect the civil rights of all its citizens.

continued to work hard within the AFL-CIO union federation. Finally, in 1963 he led the movement in a March on Washington. This was the same march he had begun to plan two decades earlier.

Planning the March

In meetings and late-night telephone calls, King proposed a March on Washington. All the great civil rights organizations and labor unions would join together in a march that would appeal to the conscience of the country. At the same time, the march would pressure the federal government to act to protect the civil rights of all its citizens. Black people and white people would join together for the march. They would call it the March on Washington for Jobs and Justice. They set the date—August 28, 1963.

Organizing a march of this size would take great skill and a total time commitment. King and all the other civil rights leaders had other obligations. They could not devote all their time to the march, but they found someone who could. They delegated most of the organizational work to long-time civil rights worker Bayard Rustin.

The federal government reacted in fear to the prospect of the August 28 demonstration. Could more than 100,000 black people possibly assemble peacefully? Would they not turn to violence and rioting and looting? The city of Washington, D.C., banned liquor sales. The federal government assembled troops. Even the Washington Senators baseball team postponed scheduled games.

People across the country supported and joined the march. More than 2,000 "freedom buses" carried marchers. Thirty "freedom trains" crossed the country. One proud 82-year-old marcher bicycled all the way from Ohio. A younger man bicycled from South Dakota. Still another marcher roller-skated from Chicago to Washington.

Labor unions brought workers. College students and high school bands came. Movie stars and politicians flew in from Hollywood on a celebrity plane.

The rally began at the Washington Monument. Hundreds of thousands assembled under a blazing August sun. Joan Baez sang "Oh, Freedom." Odetta sang "I'm on My Way." Peter, Paul, and Mary sang "Blowing in the Wind."

Bayard Rustin (1912-1987)

Bayard Rustin was born in 1912 in West Chester, Pennsylvania. Although he was a brilliant student, he was forced out of college by poverty during the Great Depression. He waited tables and played music in Harlem restaurants. He also talked about revolution.

Only one political organization treated blacks and whites with strict equality. That organization was the Communist Party. During the 1930s many people believed the Communist Party was devoted to equal rights and justice for all. Bayard Rustin joined the party.

During World War II, the Communist Party ordered Rustin to stop all organizing about racial justice in order to concentrate on the defense of Russia against the Germans. Rustin could not and would not do so. Instead, he resigned from the party.

Now Rustin offered his talents to A. Philip Randolph, who steered the young man to the Fellowship of Reconciliation (FOR), a pacifist organization devoted to Gandhi's principles of nonviolence. Rustin worked for FOR and for the Congress of Racial Equality (CORE), which was begun by FOR.

After World War II ended, Rustin organized a "Journey of Reconciliation," an integrated group that rode south on buses to challenge segregation laws. Like the Freedom Riders who came more than a decade later, Rustin went to jail for his principles. He served a sentence on a chain gang. Although he was sometimes beaten and sometimes jailed, Rustin always seemed joyful in his involvement in the struggle.

Then he was fired from FOR and CORE. Why? Bayard Rustin was a homosexual. In those days homosexuality was illegal and a matter of deep shame to many people. When Rustin's homosexuality became publicly known, the leaders of FOR and CORE decided that they could not afford to associate with him.

Rustin had never made much money in his work for justice. The loss of a position was not a financial blow. What hurt him was the loss of trust and community. But he would not give up.

Although Rustin's youthful membership in the Communist Party and his homosexuality embarrassed many civil rights leaders, they had to recognize his genius for organizing.

A quarter of a million marchers came to Washington. Most were black. More than 60,000 white people came, too.

Recognizing the historic nature of the March on Washington, people brought even very young children to be part of the day.

Bob Dylan and the SNCC Freedom Singers took turns onstage.

A quarter of a million marchers came to Washington. Most were black. More than 60,000 white people came, too. The crowd marched toward the Lincoln Memorial. They covered the grass on both sides of the half-mile reflecting pool.

Backstage, speakers argued until the rally began. Some wanted to voice their anger at the weak actions of the federal government. Some wanted to shout in anger over the long denial of their rights as human beings. Others urged caution and conciliation. They feared that anger would "turn off" white support for the civil rights bill that was to come before Congress.

The speakers at the march covered a range of American life. A. Philip Randolph was a key leader and organizer of the march. The other official leaders of the march were Martin Luther King, Jr. of the SCLC, Roy Wilkins of the NAACP, Whitney Young of the Urban League (another civil rights organization), James Farmer of CORE, and John Lewis of SNCC. Walter Reuther led the mostly-white Union of Auto Workers. Reuther insisted that "We cannot defend freedom in Berlin so long as we deny freedom in Birmingham!"

Catholics were represented by Washington Archbishop Patrick O'Boyle. He offered the opening prayer. Reverend Eugene Carson Blake spoke as well. He was a prominent white minister from the National Council of Churches. Blake had once been pastor to former President Dwight Eisenhower. Blake had been arrested in a civil rights demonstration in Baltimore. Rabbi Joachim Prinz of the American Jewish Congress spoke near the end of the rally.

SNCC leader John Lewis spoke about living in fear. Lewis had grown up on a farm in Alabama. He was the only speaker who talked of "black people" rather than "Negroes." He called on people to recognize "that we are involved in a serious social revolution." He denounced politicians who "build their careers on immoral compromises and ally themselves with open forms of political, economic, and social exploitation."

The last speaker of the day was Dr. King. "We will not be satisfied," he said, "until justice runs down like waters and righteousness like a mighty stream." Dr. King himself felt moved by this quotation from the biblical prophet Amos. He left his written text. As he preached on, his most memorable words

National Archives and Records Administration

More than a quarter of a million people gathered for the March on Washington.

"I say to you today, my friends, and so even though we face the difficulties of today and tomorrow, I still have a dream. It is a dream deeply rooted in the American dream. . . ."

The March on Washington was bigger than anyone had predicted or imagined.

Where Were the Women?

Years later, Coretta Scott King wrote about the March on Washington. She wrote that she wanted to march beside her husband. The planning council of the march decided that was not to be. Only the men were to march as leaders.

"I must confess, though," she wrote, "that I felt that the involvement in the movement of some of the wives had been so extensive that they should have been granted the privilege of marching with their husbands and of completely sharing this experience together, as they had shared the dangers and hardships."

Like many talented women of that era, she had given up her own career. Instead, she made it her career to support her husband. She used her musical training to lead church choirs. Using her superb voice, she gave freedom concerts to benefit SCLC. Her talents were used to support her husband and the movement.

The wives were essential to the Civil Rights Movement. Their strength supported the men. They gave words and ideas to their husbands—and received none of the glory. Even when they wanted to, they could not march or risk jail. Coretta and Martin agreed that she would not risk jail. They had young children. Someone had to take care of the children. He would march. He would be arrested. She would not.

So, when the time for recognition came, Martin was recognized. Coretta was not.

poured out: "I say to you today, my friends, and so even though we face the difficulties of today and tomorrow, I still have a dream. It is a dream deeply rooted in the American dream. . . ."

The March on Washington was bigger than anyone had predicted or imagined. Civil rights leaders insisted that it was a sign. They said it showed widespread American support for equality and justice. Politicians were not so sure.

A civil rights bill had been introduced in Congress. Civil rights leaders wanted to make it a strong bill. They wanted guarantees of equal rights in voting, employment, housing, education, and public accommodations. (Public accommodations include restaurants, buses and trains, stores, and so on.) Congress resisted. Southern Democrats and others opposed integration. In order to prevent a vote on the bill, they gave speeches that went on for hours and hours, sometimes including reading lists of names from a telephone directory. They used every tactic possible to stall the bill. Parliamentary maneuvering and debate went on and on. (This delaying strategy is called a *filibuster*.)

After the March

As 1963 drew to a close, two explosions shook the country. The first, in September, killed four young girls in Birmingham. The second was the assassination of President Kennedy in Dallas, Texas, on November 22. The violence of these events challenged the faith of many, but the movement continued.

National Archives and Records Administration

Martin Luther King, Jr. gave his famous "I Have a Dream" speech at the March on Washington.

Recital Day

In May, as each school's year drew to a close, students in small country schools prepared for a recital day or performance day. On this day they would stand up in front of an audience of their classmates and parents and recite speeches or poetry that they had learned by heart. The Declaration of Independence and the Gettysburg Address were favorites of many, as well as dramatic poetry readings of "Hiawatha," "The Highwayman," and "What is so rare as a day in June?"

Directions

For your civil rights performance day, recruit some friends to be performers with you. Decide on one person to be the master of ceremonies, who will introduce each recital. Choose and memorize recital pieces.

Invite friends, relatives, and neighbors to come to your Civil Rights Recital Day. To make the occasion more festive, serve cookies and lemonade to all!

Here are some suggestions for recital pieces.

What to the American Slave Is Your Fourth of July?

A speech delivered by Frederick Douglass on July 4, 1852, in Rochester, New York

[This is an excerpt from the full speech.]

Fellow Citizens: Pardon me, and allow me to ask, why am I called to speak here today? What have I or those I represent to do with your national independence? Are the great principles of political freedom and natural justice, embodied in that Declaration of Independence, extended to us? And am I, therefore, called upon to bring our humble offering to the national altar, and to confess the benefits, and express devout gratitude for the blessings resulting from your independence to us?

Would to God, both for your sakes and ours, that an affirmative answer could be truthfully returned to these questions. Then would my task be light, and my burden easy and delightful. . . .

But such is not the state of the case. I say it with a sad sense of disparity between us.

I am not included within the pale of this glorious anniversary. Your high independence only reveals the immeasurable distance between us. The blessings in which you this day rejoice are not enjoyed in common. The rich inheritance of justice, liberty, prosperity, and independence bequeathed by your fathers is shared by you, not by me. The sunlight that brought life and healing to you has brought stripes and death to me. This Fourth of July is yours, not mine. You may rejoice, I must mourn. To drag a man in fetters into the grand illuminated temple of liberty, and call upon him to join you in joyous anthems, were inhuman mockery and sacrilegious irony. Do you mean, citizens, to mock me, by asking me to speak today?

What to the American slave is your Fourth of July? I answer, a day that reveals to him more than all other days of the year, the gross injustice and cruelty to which he is the constant victim. To him your celebration is a sham; your boasted liberty an unholy license; your national greatness, swelling vanity; your sounds of rejoicing are empty and heartless; your denunciation of tyrants, brass-fronted impudence; your shouts of liberty and equality, hollow mockery; your prayers and hymns, your sermons and thanksgivings, with all your religious parade and solemnity, are to him mere bombast, fraud, deception, impiety, and hypocrisy's thin veil to cover up crimes which would disgrace a nation of savages. There is not a nation of the earth guilty of practices more shocking and bloody than are the people of these United States at this very hour.

Go where you may, search where you will, roam through all the monarchies and despotisms of the Old World, travel through South America, search out every abuse and when you have found the last, lay your facts by the side of the every day practices of this nation, and you will say with me that, for revolting barbarity and shameless hypocrisy, America reigns without a rival.

Ain't I a Woman?

Speech delivered by Sojourner Truth in 1851 at the Women's Convention in Akron, Ohio

Well, children, where there is so much racket there must be something out of kilter. I think that 'twixt the negroes of the South and the women of the North, all talking about rights, the white men will be in a fix pretty soon. But what's all this here talking about?

That man over there says that women need to be helped into carriages, and lifted over ditches, and to have the best place everywhere. Nobody ever helps me into carriages, or over mudpuddles, or gives me any best place! And ain't I a woman?

Look at me! Look at my arm! I have ploughed and planted, and gathered into barns, and no man could head me! And ain't I a woman? I could work as much and eat as much as a man—when I could get it—and bear the lash as well! And ain't I a woman? I have borne thirteen children, and seen most all sold off to slavery, and when I cried out with my mother's grief, none but Jesus heard me! And ain't I a woman?

Then they talk about this thing in the head; what's this they call it? That's it, honey. What's that got to do with women's rights or negroes' rights? If my cup won't hold but a pint, and yours holds a quart, wouldn't you be mean not to let me have my little half measure full?

Then that little man in black there, he says women can't have as much rights as men, 'cause Christ wasn't a woman! Where did your Christ come from? Where did your Christ come from? From God and a woman! Man had nothing to do with Him.

If the first woman God ever made was strong enough to turn the world upside down all alone, these women together ought to be able to turn it back, and get it right side up again! And now they is asking to do it, the men better let them.

Obliged to you for hearing me, and now old Sojourner ain't got nothing more to say.

For other great readings, look for poems by Langston Hughes, Gwendolyn Brooks, Amiri Baraka, Nikki Giovanni, Ntozake Shange, and other African American poets.

Demonstrate Your Commitment

Have you ever wanted to march or demonstrate? Here's your chance! You can make signs to carry in a march or demonstration. Then you can carry or wear them on a special occasion. With any luck at all, you won't even get arrested.

Materials

Poster board
String
Colored markers
Rulers

Directions

Even if you were born too late for the civil rights marches of the 1960s, you still have lots of opportunities to demonstrate your own commitment. If you are really ambitious, you can organize your own march for a special occasion, such as the 4th of July or Martin Luther King Day. But it is probably easier to get an audience if you join an already-organized march. You might join in a 4th of July parade as a new marching unit. In some cities there are marches

on Martin Luther King Day that would welcome your participation. If it's too cold in January for an outdoor march, your school might sponsor an indoor parade.

Be sure to recruit friends (and maybe even relatives) to march with you. While one person can demonstrate, more people deliver the message more effectively.

Once you know where and when you are marching, it's time to make your signs. Schedule an afternoon or evening for sign-making.

Make up your own slogans and drawings for the signs, or adapt some that have been used before:

- Freedom Now

- Black and White Together

- Integrate Our Schools

- Justice for All

If you are marching on the 4th of July, you might want to include a flag in your design. If you are marching on Dr. King's birthday, you might include a drawing of Dr. King. Be creative!

If you look at news photos of early civil rights marches, you will see people holding signs in front of them, or wearing sandwich signs, one in front and one in back. If you decide on sandwich signs, just punch holes in the signs at least one inch from the top, and tie them together with string, adjusting the length of the string so that they hang right.

Now you are ready to march!

"Praying with My Feet"

Religion and Civil Rights

"Praying with My Feet"

Introduction

Throughout the Civil Rights Movement, religion played a crucial part. Perhaps a majority of the people working and demonstrating for civil rights were inspired and strengthened by their religious convictions. Although many of these people belonged to different churches and different religions, they shared a common belief in the equality of all human beings.

Some of the violence directed at the Civil Rights Movement targeted churches and religious people. Religious faith gave these people strength to persevere in spite of suffering and danger.

Birmingham Sunday

On the morning of September 15, 1963, people gathered at Birmingham's Sixteenth Street Baptist Church. Young girls dressed in white from head to toe. Today was their day to shine. Young people always led the annual Youth Day services.

Carole Robertson and Cynthia Wesley, both 14 years old, combed their hair in a downstairs bathroom. Addie Mae Collins, also 14, retied a sash for 11-year-old Denise McNair. She got the bow just right. The friends giggled together. They admired themselves in the mirror.

The older people were upstairs. The women's Sunday School discussion went on. Today's topic was "The Love That Forgives." A hum of eager voices came from the group. Class was almost over. Suddenly, the women heard an explosion. They felt the church rock on its foundations.

Twelve-year-old Sarah Collins stumbled through the broken church wall. Blood ran from her nose and ears. She could barely see. An ambulance took her away.

Her big sister was not so lucky. Addie Mae died in the church basement. So did her three friends. Four young girls became four more martyrs of the Civil Rights Movement. They were killed by a bomb intended to kill and frighten black people committed to the Civil Rights Movement.

Bombing black churches was nothing new. In Birmingham alone at least 20 bombs had hit churches and homes of civil rights leaders. Across the South, African American churches

Today the four young girls who died in the Birmingham church bombing are commemorated in a memorial that bears their photos.

were targets. Some were bombed. Some were burned to the ground.

Religion was central to African American life and culture. It had been since slavery days. Preachers and churches helped struggling people. They helped communities to survive. Civil rights meetings were held in churches. Churches were the only place black people could meet in the South. Churches were a place for civil rights in the North as well. That is why white racists targeted the churches.

Leaders of the Civil Rights Movement, such as King, Abernathy, and Shuttlesworth, came from churches. The honor roll goes on and on. Many student leaders, like James Bevel, studied for the ministry. Some became ministers. Others left school to devote their lives to the struggle for justice. Religious faith inspired them to give their lives to the movement.

Minister and Rabbi Together

People of different religions found common ground in the movement. Catholics joined Protestants. Jews joined Christians.

Rabbi Abraham Heschel was a renowned Jewish scholar and writer. He was born in Warsaw, Poland, in 1907. An Orthodox Jew, he was the descendant of generations of famous rabbis. He taught courses on Jewish philosophy and theology at universities in Berlin and Frankfurt before the Nazis took power.

Fleeing Hitler's Holocaust, Rabbi Heschel came to the United States. In 1945 he accepted a position as a professor at the Jewish Theological Seminary in New York. He continued there until his death in 1972.

In the 1960s Rabbi Heschel entered into a dialogue with the Catholic Church. Pope John XXIII had called a Vatican Council of the world's Catholic bishops. Rabbi Heschel secretly consulted with Catholic leaders. They discussed Catholic anti-Semitism. He asked that they speak out against anti-Jewish prejudices. He wanted them to make clear that the Catholic Church did not hold Jews responsible for the death of Jesus. Rabbi Heschel's consultation with the Catholics was controversial for many Catholics and Jews.

Rabbi Heschel's advocacy of civil rights was also controversial to many. For Heschel it was a commitment required by his faith. He believed that social action was the way for a religious person to express ethical beliefs.

In January 1963 Rabbi Heschel met Dr. King in Chicago. Both spoke at a national conference on race and religion.

"Religion and race," preached Heschel. "How can the two be uttered together? To act in the spirit of religion is to unite what lies apart, to remember that humanity as a whole is God's beloved child. To act in the spirit of race is to sunder, to slash, to dismember the flesh of living humanity. . . ."

King challenged white Christians. "Eleven o'clock on Sunday morning is still America's most segregated hour," he preached, "and the Sunday School is still the most segregated school of the week." Conference participants recognized the problem of racism. King said that was not enough. "One must not only preach a sermon with his voice," said King. "He must preach it with his life."

King and Heschel drew on common roots of both Jewish and Christian religious teaching. Both recalled the words of the biblical prophets. They summoned people of faith to remember. They begged people to take seriously the prophets' calls for justice. Both quoted the words of the prophet Amos: "Let justice roll down like waters, and righteousness like a mighty stream."

Religious people responded to the call. They joined the movement. They went to marches, demonstrations, and jail cells. When they needed help, civil rights leaders called northern seminaries. They called college chaplains. People of faith came to the front lines.

Religious leaders were prominent in the Civil Rights Movement.

People of Faith in Florida

In the spring of 1964, St. Augustine, Florida, was a battleground. The black community suffered. Their children sat in jail for months on end. Bombers set fire to their homes. Carloads of gun-toting white teens invaded their communities. Night riders with guns shot up civil rights leaders' homes. Negroes in St. Augustine sent out a call for help.

Hundreds of white students and chaplains went south to Florida. Three northern Episcopal bishops were invited. The Florida Episcopal bishop did not want them to come, so the northern bishops turned down the invitation.

The three bishops' wives were moved by their own religious faith. They went south in place of their husbands. Mary Peabody was the wife of Bishop Malcolm Peabody. She was also the mother of Massachusetts governor Endicott Peabody, and grandmother of seven. Esther Burgess, wife of Bishop John Burgess, was a black woman. Peabody and Burgess sat down together at a Florida lunch counter. They were ordered to leave.

Mary Peabody was shocked. She had expected that white people would be polite and reasonable. The people in the restaurant were neither.

At least, she thought, church people would be different. They would show her courtesy. On

Members of the Nation of Islam preached resistance and self-defense.

Sunday morning she tried to attend services at Trinity Episcopal Church in St. Augustine. Instead of services, she found a closed door. The church had canceled services to keep the bishops' wives out.

Burgess was the first of the bishops' wives to be arrested. The next day, Peabody followed her to jail. Local women and northern students went to jail, too. Peabody's jailing brought immediate and massive media attention.

The Freedom Summer of 1964 heated up. Dr. King went to St. Augustine and to jail. From the jail, King wrote to Rabbi Israel Dressler. He pleaded for support.

Rabbi Dressler took the letter to a convention of rabbis. Sixteen rabbis and one lay leader from eight different states left immediately for Florida. The day after they arrived, they tried to integrate a restaurant. Police arrested all of them. They spent that day and night in jail. In jail they met black ministers and movement leaders.

Jews, Catholics, and Protestants did not share the same religious beliefs. They did share a commitment to justice for all, regardless of race. Baptists, Methodists, Catholics, Jews, Muslims—they joined together to work for civil rights. Together they walked, lived, laughed, and prayed. Together, they even gave their lives for the cause.

The Nation of Islam

The Nation of Islam was founded by Elijah Muhammad. He taught that black people were the children of God. He taught that white people were devils. Muhammad ridiculed the nonviolence of the Civil Rights Movement.

Members of the Nation of Islam were also called Black Muslims. They preached resistance and self-defense. They followed strict discipline in all matters—from what they ate to how they dressed in public. Men wore short hair and dark suits. Women covered their heads and wore long dresses. Muslims could not drink alcohol or use drugs.

Muhammad organized the Nation of Islam in a military manner. All Muslims followed strict lines of command. Black Muslim men were encouraged to own guns. They carried guns for self-defense. Police across the country feared Black Muslims. Black Muslims considered police their enemies. They said police were instruments of white oppression.

The undeniable courage of the Civil Rights Movement inspired respect among many Black Muslims. One of them was the fiery preacher Malcolm X.

Like many Black Muslims, Malcolm X was converted to the Nation of Islam while in prison. He became a devout Muslim and therefore never again smoked, drank, or ate pork. In 1952 Malcolm was released from prison. He gave up his "slave name" of Malcolm Little and renamed himself Malcolm X. The X stood for the identity of which he and other African Americans had been robbed by slave traders and slave masters.

Malcolm was an eloquent preacher. Although he felt uneasy about some of Muhammad's actions, he swallowed his doubts. He supported Muhammad as the leader of the Nation of Islam. Then came a turning point in his life.

In 1964 Malcolm made a pilgrimage to Mecca. For the first time, he found himself in

How You'll Get Your Freedom

Speaking in 1964, Malcolm X talked about how people would be set free by working together.

the company of thousands of other believers in Islam. Many of them were white. He was received as a brother. He began to wonder about Elijah Muhammad's blanket condemnation of all white people as devils.

Malcolm X returned to the United States as an orthodox Muslim. He founded the Organization for Afro-American Unity. He became even a bigger celebrity than before his pilgrimage. He also found greater distance and distrust between himself and Muhammad.

After leaving the Nation of Islam because of disagreements with Elijah Muhammad, Malcolm X drew closer to the Civil Rights Movement, though he still maintained that nonviolence would not work. "It is criminal to teach a man not to defend himself when he is the constant victim of brutal attacks," Malcolm insisted.

You'll get freedom by letting your enemy know that you'll do anything to get your freedom; then you'll get it. It's the only way you'll get it. When you get that kind of attitude, they'll label you as a "crazy Negro," or they'll call you a "crazy nigger"—they don't say Negro. Or they'll call you an extremist or a subversive, or seditious, or a red, or a radical. But when you stay radical long enough and get enough people to be like you, you'll get your freedom.

Malcolm eventually separated from Elijah Muhammad, though not from the religion of Islam. He remained a devout Muslim his whole life.

In 1965 Malcolm X was assassinated. The assassins shot him down as he spoke to an audience in New York City. Many people believe the killers were connected to the Nation of Islam.

Division Within the Churches

Across the South, black churches gave a home to the Civil Rights Movement. Meetings were

held in black churches. Black ministers led the movement. Black hymns and spirituals gave voice to marchers and to prisoners in jails.

Not all black churches supported the Civil Rights Movement. Some were quite conservative. Some opposed any action that broke the law. Some said that black people should "go slow" and "stop pushing so hard." Their leaders said the movement was too political, too worldly, for religious people.

Many southern white churches strongly defended segregation. These churches were segregated, too. Their members refused to allow black people to worship with them.

Theology and economics help explain the religious differences over civil rights. Theology explains what people believe about God and religion. Economics tells where people's financial interest lies.

In conservative churches, ministers preached that suffering was the way to salvation. Black people suffered in this world. They would be rewarded in heaven.

In activist churches, ministers emphasized Christian love and justice. They preached that all people were equal as children of God. They focused on God leading the Hebrew people out of slavery and into freedom. Their theology led them into the Civil Rights Movement.

Economic interests are also important. Many black ministers had more money than the people they led. Sometimes, they received more respect from white people. Sometimes they did not want to risk their position in the community. Being part of the Civil Rights Movement was always a risky business. Other churches and ministers risked everything. Some of them paid with their lives.

Working Side by Side

Leadership in the Civil Rights Movement came from religious people. So did much of the time and energy needed for the hard, unglamorous, daily work. In that work religious people worked side by side with nonbelievers. Each learned to value the person and contributions of the other. The movement umbrella was wide enough to cover ministers in dark suits, white shirts, and ties and hippies wearing love beads and tattered blue jeans.

Journalists focused on the big leaders and big stories of the movement. Many of the stories of ordinary people inspired by the Civil Rights Movement remain to be told.

Many of the stories of ordinary people inspired by the Civil Rights Movement remain to be told.

Record Oral Histories

Oral history is a way of learning about a time in history by talking to people who lived through that time. You can interview people in your family, people in your neighborhood, or other acquaintances. Then you can write stories or reports based on your interviews. Your writing could be published in a local newspaper or in a school publication!

Do you know anyone who remembers the Civil Rights Movement of the 1950s and 1960s? Were they excited by the changes that came with the movement? Perhaps your great-uncle or your grandmother remembers watching Martin Luther King, Jr. on television. Maybe your great-aunt took part in a protest or demonstration. Maybe your minister was active in a civil rights organization. Maybe you know people who were angered or frightened by the changes that came with the Civil Rights Movement. What do they remember most vividly?

Materials

Notebook

Pencils

Tape recorder

Cassettes

Extension cord or batteries

Directions

While you can conduct oral history interviews by yourself, working with a partner might be more fun. You and your partner can begin by choosing two or three people whom you would like to interview. Ask them if they would be willing to talk to you about their memories of the Civil Rights Movement in the 1960s.

Once you have identified your interviewees, conduct a pre-interview. (This can be done in person or by telephone.) Ask a few questions so that you know what you can talk about during the interview. You might ask:

1. How old were you during the 1960s?

2. Where did you live?

3. What is the earliest thing you remember about the Civil Rights Movement?

4. What events do you remember as most important to you?

After you know a little about the person you will interview, make an appointment for the interview itself. During the pre-interview ask whether you may tape record the interview.

Before the actual interview, make a list of questions that you can use. Start with easy questions, and include some questions that help people remember significant events. Here are some starter questions:

1. How did you hear about the 1963 March on Washington? Dr. King's "I Have a Dream" speech? What do you remember thinking or saying about the event?

2. What do you remember hearing about segregated schools? Can you remember any conversations about segregation?

3. Did you participate in the Civil Rights Movement—by marching, by writing letters, or in any other way? What did you do?

4. Did you know anyone else who participated in the Civil Rights Movement? What do you remember about them?

Organizing your questions ahead of time will help make the interview go smoothly. If you are very familiar with your questions, then you can leave out some of them or skip ahead to other questions during the interview, depending on what stories people tell you.

Before you conduct the interview, assemble your equipment: notebooks and pencils, tape recorder and tapes, extension cord or batteries. (Or, if you are really ambitious, a video camera and tripod!) Try out your recording equipment ahead of time, so that you know how to work it and how to set volume levels.

Finally, you are ready for the interview! This is the big event. Remember to listen carefully to what she or he has to say, to let the interviewee do most of the talking, and to thank the interviewee.

After your interviews, use your notes and the tape recording to produce a report or a story, including the most interesting parts of the interview. Think about how to share your finished oral history. Could you use it as a classroom report? Could you publish it in a school or local newspaper?

Freedom Singers

In this activity, you will keep alive the songs of the Civil Rights Movement by forming a group of freedom singers.

Civil rights activists and sympathizers alike sang the stirring hymns and folk songs of the movement. They sang in rallies and gatherings, sang while marching down the street or picketing stores, sang while being carried off to jail in police wagons. Their songs reached through prison bars and connected them to one another. In the jail in Rock Hill, South Carolina, in 1961, imprisoned student demonstrators sang so strongly that the sheriff tried, unsuccessfully, to stop the music by putting them in solitary confinement.

Some songs had roots that reached back to slavery. Others were composed or adapted especially for the Civil Rights Movement. All of them became the property of the people who sang them.

Hollis Watkins, who was involved in the early days of the movement, explains: "[S]inging music is an integral part of Southern black people's lives. So, it's deeply embedded into the culture. So the reason this was so important is

National Archives and Records Administration

Singing both expressed and strengthened the spirit of the civil rights demonstrators.

because this is something that black people could relate to."

All you need for this activity is three or four people, though thousands can join in these songs of freedom. You can find songs of the 1960s on compact discs and tapes. Here are a few to get you started.

"We Shall Overcome"

The composer of this song is unknown, but the lyrics are derived from Charles Tindley's gospel song "I'll Overcome Some Day" (1900), and the opening and closing melody from the nineteenth-century spiritual "No More Auction Block for Me" (a song that predates the Civil War).

We shall overcome,
We shall overcome,
We shall overcome some day.
Oh, deep in my heart,
I do believe
We shall overcome some day.

(Other verses:
We'll walk hand in hand . . .
Black and white together . . .
We shall live in peace . . .
We shall all be free . . .)

"Like a Tree Planted by the Water"

This is a traditional song.

We shall not, we shall not be moved!
We shall not, we shall not be moved!
Just like a tree that's planted by the water,
We shall not be moved!

Fighting for our freedom, we shall not
    be moved!
Fighting for our freedom, we shall not
    be moved!
Just like a tree that's planted by the water,
We shall not be moved!

Black and white together, we shall not
    be moved!
Black and white together, we shall not
    be moved!
Just like a tree that's planted by the water,
We shall not be moved!

"Oh, Freedom Over Me"

This is a Negro spiritual that predates the Civil War.

Oh, freedom! Oh, freedom!

Oh, freedom over me!
And before I'll be a slave, I'll be buried in
*   my grave,*
And go home to my Lord and be free!

No more weeping, no more weeping,
No more weeping over me!
And before I'll be a slave, I'll be buried in
*   my grave,*
And go home to my Lord and be free!

No segregation, no segregation,
No segregation over me!
And before I'll be a slave, I'll be buried in
*   my grave,*
And go home to my Lord and be free!

"Lift Every Voice and Sing"

This hymn, written in 1900 by James Weldon Johnson for a presentation in celebration of Abraham Lincoln's birthday, has become known as "The Negro National Anthem."

Lift every voice and sing

Till earth and heaven ring,
Ring with the harmonies of liberty;
Let our rejoicing rise
High as the listening skies,
Let it resound loud as the rolling sea.
Sing a song full of the faith that the dark
*   past has taught us,*
Sing a song full of the hope that the present
*   has brought us,*
Facing the rising sun of our new day
*   begun*
Let us march on till victory is won.

Stony the road we trod
Bitter the chastening rod,
Felt in the days when hope unborn had died;
Yet with a steady beat
Have not our weary feet
Come to the place for which our
*   fathers sighed?*
We have come over a way that with
*   tears has been watered,*
We have come, treading our path
*   through the blood of the slaughtered,*
Out from the gloomy past,

Till now we stand at last
Where the white gleam of our bright star
    is cast.

God of our weary years,
God of our silent tears.
Thou who has brought us thus far on
    the way;
Thou who has by Thy might
Led us into the light,
Keep us forever in the path, we pray.
Lest our feet stray from the places,
Our God, where we met Thee;
Lest, our hearts drunk with the wine of
    the world, we forget Thee;
Shadowed beneath Thy hand,
May we forever stand.
True to our God.
True to our native land.

"This Little Light of Mine"

Harry Dixon Loes wrote the words and music
for this famous spiritual.

This little light of mine, I'm gonna let
    it shine!
This little light of mine, I'm gonna let
    it shine!
This little light of mine, I'm gonna let
    it shine—
Let it shine, let it shine, let it shine!

All over this country, I'm gonna let it shine!
All over this country, I'm gonna let it shine!
All over this country, I'm gonna let it shine!
Let it shine, let it shine, let it shine!

On all of God's children, I'm gonna let
    it shine!
On all of God's children, I'm gonna let
    it shine!
On all of God's children, I'm gonna let
    it shine!
Let it shine, let it shine, let it shine!

This little light of freedom, I'm gonna let
    it shine!
This little light of freedom, I'm gonna let
    it shine!

This little light of freedom, I'm gonna let
*   it shine!*
Let it shine, let it shine, let it shine!

(Make up your own verses.)

"He's Got the Whole World in His Hands"

This is a Negro spiritual that predates the Civil
War.

He's got the whole world in His hands,
He's got the whole world in His hands,
He's got the whole world in His hands,
He's got the whole world in His hands.

He's got you and me, brother, in His hands.
He's got you and me, sister, in His hands.
He's got you and me, brother, in His hands.
He's got the whole world in His hands.

He's got black and white, brother, in
*   His hands.*
He's got black and white, sister, in
*   His hands.*

He's got black and white, brother, in
*   His hands.*
He's got the whole world in His
*   hands.*

"Swing Low, Sweet Chariot"

Swing low, sweet chariot,
Coming for to carry me home!
Swing low, sweet chariot,
Coming for to carry me home.

I looked over Jordan and what
*   did I see?*
Coming for to carry me home!
A band of angels coming after me,
Coming for to carry me home.

"When the Saints Go Marching In"

Oh, when the saints go marching in,
Oh, when the saints go marching in,
Oh, Lord, I want to be in that
*   number,*
When the saints go marching in!

Oh, when that glory day is here,
Oh, when that glory day is here,
Oh, Lord, I want to be in that number,
When the saints go marching in!

Oh, when that new world is revealed,
Oh, when that new world is revealed,
Oh, Lord, I want to be in that number,
When the saints go marching in!

HE'S GOT THE WHOLE WORLD IN HIS HANDS...

Love Beads

You can create a unique piece of jewelry in the style of the hippies and flower power days of the 1960s.

Materials

Clay

Wax paper or foil

Toothpicks and/or needles

Acrylic paints

Clear acrylic finish

String or thread

Directions

Beads are easy to make. Just roll clay into balls. You can make all your beads a uniform size and shape, or you can vary them. You may want to make a peace symbol or a cross or a star for the center piece of your necklace. If you do, be sure to leave a clay "handle" at the top, so you will have a place to run the string through it.

When you have made 20 or 30 or more beads, depending on the number you want on your necklace, line them all up on wax paper or foil. Using a toothpick or a needle, make a hole all the way through the center of the bead. Remember to make a hole in your peace symbol, too! Let the beads air-dry or bake them in the oven, following the directions for the particular kind of clay you are using.

After the beads are dry, paint them in the colors of your choice. If you want multicolored beads, let the first coat dry completely before applying a second color. After all the beads are completely dry, give them a final coat of clear acrylic finish.

Arrange the beads on the wax paper or foil in the shape of the necklace you want to create. Then string them in order on the thread or string of your choice. Cut the string long enough so that, when knotted, you can just slip it on and off over your head.

Voilà! You have a love bead necklace!

"You May Be Killed"

Freedom Summer, 1964

"You May Be Killed"

Introduction

The year of 1963 had been filled with death and destruction. Churches were bombed. Students were bloodied. Children were murdered. Leaders were assassinated. Through it all, the Civil Rights Movement continued. None of these tragedies could stop the determined march toward freedom.

Northern ministers and college students and others watched the Civil Rights Movement on television and were inspired by the words and examples of its leaders. They wanted to help. Some had already gone to the South to join the work. The summer of 1964 would bring an even larger migration of northern volunteers to the South.

Freedom Days

On January 22, 1964, Hattiesburg, Mississippi, observed Freedom Day. SNCC worked to register voters in the state. On Freedom Day, SNCC planned an all-out attempt to register black voters in Hattiesburg. Organizers sent an urgent summons to supporters. Fifty-some northern white ministers, priests, and rabbis answered the call. Reporters and movement leaders also showed. On the eve of Freedom Day, they gathered at a mass meeting.

The next morning, for the very first time, Mississippi police followed orders to protect the demonstrators. A picket line of demonstrators marched in the rain. Prospective voters lined up. One by one, they applied for registration. Freedom Day stayed quiet. With no blood or violence to report, the media paid little attention.

Picket lines and registration continued. More northern clergy arrived to take the places of the first group. Those who returned home told stories of southern segregation. They praised the bravery of freedom fighters. They inspired others to follow their example.

Segregation in the North

At the same time, part of the focus of the Civil Rights Movement shifted. Now civil rights leaders turned to the North.

In the South, laws and police enforced segregation. In the North, housing and schools were just as segregated. Northern segregation was by custom and not by law. In Chicago, for example, no law ordered school and housing segregation. Long-standing custom kept neighborhoods and schools strictly segregated.

Even in the North segregation was enforced by threats and violence. Usually, African American families were kept out of "white" neighborhoods because no one would sell them a home. If an African American family moved into a white neighborhood, they met danger. They might find a cross burning on their lawn. Sometimes bricks were thrown through their windows. Their children faced harassment on the street and in schools.

In New York City schools were segregated. School segregation resulted from segregated housing. Black people lived in many Harlem neighborhoods. Schools in these neighborhoods served mostly black students. These schools offered clearly inferior education.

In the spring of 1964 Bayard Rustin organized a one-day boycott of New York City schools. Some 400,000 African American students stayed home.

J. Edgar Hoover and the Federal Bureau of Investigation (FBI) already opposed the Civil Rights Movement in the South. Although the federal government was often called on to enforce desegregation laws and to protect black people in the South, not all federal officials agreed with this policy. Hoover and the FBI often resisted the orders of the U.S. Justice Department. Hoover hated King and the Civil Rights Movement. Now they gleefully spread stories calling Bayard Rustin a communist. They claimed that the school boycott was a communist plot.

Many northern whites supported an end to segregation-by-law in the South, but they did not want to end segregation-in-fact in their own schools or neighborhoods. The FBI smear campaign against civil rights leaders gave them an excuse for their reluctance. Northern white backlash against the Civil Rights Movement grew.

Freedom Summer in Mississippi

The Civil Rights Movement spread across the entire nation. Civil rights activists in Mississippi

Although the federal government was often called on to enforce desegregation laws and to protect black people in the South, not all federal officials agreed with this policy.

One of the elder

civil rights

leaders who had

long been active in

literacy and voter

education was

Septima Clark.

began to plan their own Freedom Summer. Freedom Summer would bring thousands of white volunteers to Mississippi. They would work with experienced black activists to register voters.

Which was the best civil rights organization? Who was the greatest leader? Questions like these could divide the civil rights community. Jealousy among leaders could stop the important organizing work.

SCLC was led by Dr. King. CORE was led by James Farmer. SNCC was young. Many thought it was radical. The NAACP was old. Many thought it was too conservative.

In Mississippi people tried to stop these divisions. They knew that they had to work together. All four organizations joined together as the Council of Federated Organizations (COFO). As COFO, they would organize a voter registration drive in Mississippi.

Forming COFO did not stop the jealousy entirely. Each group sometimes felt that another was getting too much credit. However, COFO did give them a way to work together. United, they faced the violence of white Mississippi.

One of the elder civil rights leaders who had

National Archives and Records Administration

Freedom Summer succeeded because of the commitment of people of all ages.

long been active in literacy and voter education was Septima Clark. Born in 1898, she had lived under segregation all her life, and she had challenged the system at every opportunity. A teacher since the age of 18, Clark began fighting for equal pay for black and white school teachers in 1935. With the assistance of NAACP lawyer Thurgood Marshall, her efforts won a court order for equal pay in 1942. As a member of the NAACP, she continued to work for justice. Then, in 1956, South Carolina passed a new law saying that no teacher could be a member of the NAACP. Clark refused to resign her membership, so she was fired.

Working for the Highlander Folk School, she began setting up citizenship schools across the South. The schools taught black adults to read so that they could register to vote.

Though whites harassed the people who ran the citizenship schools, they continued with their work. "There were 897 [schools] going from 1957 to 1970," Clark remembers. "They were in people's kitchens, in beauty parlors, and under trees in the summertime. I went all over the South, sometimes visiting three citizenship schools in one day, checking to be sure they weren't using textbooks, but were teaching people to read those election laws and to write their names in cursive writing."

The citizenship schools played an important part in the Voter Education Project. Almost

A Voice of Hope

As an older woman, Septima Clark looked back on her long life of service. She spoke with hope.

As we go along, it's going to take that hundred years for attitudes to change. They will change. . . . I don't expect to ever see a utopia. No, I think there will always be something that you're going to have to work on, always. . . . The only thing that's really worthwhile is change. It's coming.

700,000 black voters registered in the South from 1962 to 1965. Another million black voters registered after the Voting Rights Act passed in 1965.

At 66 years of age, Clark was a shining example of the older generation of committed black activists. Michael and Rita Schwerner were among the younger generation whose commitment and energy inspired this Freedom Summer. This young New York couple made a commitment to full-time work with the movement. They came to the South in January and opened a CORE community center in Meridian, Mississippi.

In May and June, schools and colleges let out for the summer. Thousands of other volunteers headed to the South. They were inspired by the Freedom Summer promise. They wanted to work in literacy and voter education campaigns. They believed deeply in the equality of all people. They shared a desire for justice.

For many, their first stop was the Western College for Women in Oxford, Ohio. Some 800 young people arrived there for a one-week SNCC orientation. They had to bring money for living expenses. They also had to bring $500 for bail. They listened as SNCC's James Forman told them: "I may be killed. You may be killed. The whole staff may go."

On June 20, 1964, the first 200 volunteers left Ohio. They set out to travel into the heart of violence. They came to rural Mississippi and Alabama, to towns where no black person had been allowed to vote since the decade following the Civil War. They lived with black families. These families risked their own lives by opening their homes to the volunteers. In letters home, volunteers described their life-changing encounters with committed, courageous families and fellow volunteers.

Chaney, Goodman, and Schwerner

Three of these first two hundred volunteers went missing on June 21, 1964. James Chaney, Andrew Goodman, and Michael Schwerner disappeared. COFO workers followed their own emergency procedures. They checked jails and called friends, the FBI, and reporters. Through the night, tension built. Morning dawned with no word of the missing volunteers. Then a jailer said that they had been in his custody some time the previous evening. Neshoba County Sheriff Rainey admitted that he and his deputy had held the three civil rights workers on a speeding ticket. He said they kept the volunteers in jail for six hours and released them after dark.

The FBI found the burned-out car that Schwerner had driven. Families and friends knew there was no hope left. The three young men were dead.

Through the long, hot summer weeks, the search for their bodies continued. As they searched, FBI agents found the bodies of three lynched black men. These men had been missing for a longer time. Finally, on August 4, the bodies of the three murdered civil rights workers were found.

The murders did not stop Freedom Summer. Nor did the constant harassment of other volunteers. The many shootings, the frequent beatings, and arrests could not stop the movement. Volunteers taught in Freedom Schools. They provided health care in Freedom Clinics. They gave legal advice in legal clinics.

Freedom Democrats

Freedom Summer focused on voter registration. Once voters were registered, they wanted to participate. The Mississippi Democratic Party would not let them in. So Freedom Summer started a new party that would let all people participate. They called it the Mississippi Freedom Democratic Party. The Mississippi Freedom Democrats selected 68 delegates, including 4 white people. The delegates wanted to represent the state at the Democratic National Convention. Their leader was Fannie Lou Hamer (1917–1977).

In 1962, at the age of 44, Fannie Lou Hamer attended her first SNCC meeting. The students organizing the voter registration drive were

SNCC's Growing Pains

As SNCC became larger, it faced internal divisions. Its early members were from the South. They based their commitment on Christian faith. Then members came from the North. Many of them shared political goals, but not religious convictions.

Young white people wanted to be part of the movement. SNCC debated their role. Should white people ever be leaders? Should white people be welcomed only if they would follow black leaders?

Then came questions of strategy. Should SNCC focus on voter registration? Or should it continue its original focus on direct action?

SNCC faced many arguments and differences of opinion. In spite of these conflicts, SNCC never lost its focus on the work of the Civil Rights Movement. SNCC members were actively present as the movement went on to Birmingham, Alabama, to Selma, and beyond.

young enough to be her children. Despite the danger, she agreed to help. "[W]hat was the point of being scared?" she said later. "The only thing they could do to me was kill me, and it seemed like they'd been trying to do that ever since I could remember."

The Hamer family lived and worked on a plantation. As soon as she tried to register to

National Archives and Records Administration

Marching for civil rights in the South required courage.

In 1963, Hamer was arrested in Winona, Mississippi. She was beaten so badly by police officers that she suffered from it the rest of her life. She described what was done to her: "They just kept beatin' me and telling me, 'You nigger bitch, we're gonna make you wish you were dead.' When they finally quit they told me to go to my cell, but I couldn't get up, I couldn't bend my knees. Every day of my life I pay with the misery of that beatin'."

The Democratic National Convention began in Atlantic City on August 22. Each state sends delegates to national party conventions. The all-white Mississippi Democrats sent delegates. The Freedom Democrats challenged the regular Mississippi delegation.

All sides negotiated. Delegates made impassioned speeches. Hamer had worked all through Mississippi's Freedom Summer to build the Mississippi Freedom Democratic Party. Now she demanded that this party's delegates be admitted to the convention, saying, "This is not Mississippi's problem. It is America's problem."

Party leaders proposed compromises. The compromises failed. The National Democratic

vote, Hamer and her husband were fired and thrown out of their house. They had no money.

Then Hamer went to work for SNCC full-time. She became famous for her preaching and singing. Her theme song was "This Little Light of Mine." (See the "Freedom Singers" activities in Chapter 7 for the lyrics to this song.)

The Making of a Leader

Fannie Lou Townsend was the youngest of the 20 children of Jim and Ella Lou Townsend. Her parents worked as sharecroppers, earning only $1.25 a day.

Townsend began working in the fields when she was six years old. Her parents worked hard and saved every penny. In 1930 they rented land of their own. With the help of all their children, they also bought a tractor. Their white neighbor didn't like their success, so he poisoned their cattle, leaving the family worse off than before.

Townsend was so discouraged that she wished she was white. Her mother scolded her: "You respect yourself as a little black child. And as you grow older, respect yourself as a black woman. Then one day, other people will respect you."

After attending school through sixth grade, Townsend continued her education through bible studies at the Baptist church.

In 1944 Fannie Lou Townsend married Perry "Pap" Hamer. She had been sterilized at an early age by a white doctor who didn't even ask her permission, so she was unable to have children of her own. She and Pap Hamer adopted four daughters.

The National Democratic Party feared losing the votes of the white southerners, so they refused to seat the Freedom Democrats.

Party feared losing the votes of the white southerners, so they refused to seat the Freedom Democrats.

Then the regular Mississippi Democrats refused to accept the party platform (statement of principles). The Democratic platform included civil rights. When the Mississippi Democrats refused to accept it, they were barred from the convention. Their chairs and space were left empty.

Although they were never seated as delegates, the Mississippi Freedom Democratic Party delegates managed to find a way into the convention hall. They testified about their experiences, they stood in the space left empty by the Mississippi delegates who refused to accept

More of the Fannie Lou Hamer Legacy

All her life Hamer kept on working for justice and freedom. One of the many projects she organized was the Pig Bank. This was a livestock-raising project to help poor people get more meat to eat. Another project was the Freedom Farm Cooperative. This cooperative helped 5,000 people to grow their own food on their own land.

Fannie Lou Hamer died in 1977. The words on her headstone are words she often said: "I'm sick and tired of being sick and tired."

Although voter registration programs suffered extreme persecution by the white police and government in Mississippi, 1964 saw the passage of a national Civil Rights Act, followed in 1965 by a national Voting Rights Act. Laws alone could not abolish segregation and discrimination. Committed people continued to work to make the promise of the law a reality. [Note: The text of both of these Acts can be found at the back of this book.]

the party platform, and then they sang freedom songs.

An End of an Era

Mississippi's Freedom Summer changed forever not only the state of Mississippi, but also the entire United States. Although the Mississippi Freedom Democratic Party delegation was not seated at the Democratic convention, never again would the Democratic Party permit any of the states to exclude black people from participating in the party process.

Food Drive

After the 1962 cotton harvest, poor families in rural Mississippi were hungry. That year's harvest brought them less money than usual. They couldn't buy food or clothing. Without shoes, children could not go to school.

The Council of Federated Organizations (COFO) asked northern friends to send help. Truckloads of food arrived. Hungry people came to food lines. There they met the young civil rights workers. The workers told them about the voter registration project.

Today people still go hungry. Some of them live in or very near your own community. You can help. With your friends, you can organize a food drive for a local food bank. You could even organize a food bank at a local church or synagogue or school.

Directions

Choose your organization. Identify the food bank where you will give the collected food donations. Call and talk to one of the staff members about times and dates.

Pick the time of year for your food drive. People like to give food at Thanksgiving. But did you know that most food banks have a hard time getting through the summer? With kids home from school, families have more mouths to feed. At the same time, many people stop giving to food banks as they go on vacation.

Here are some things to keep in mind when you plan your food drive.

Any time is a good time for a food drive.

Who will help? Recruit friends or classmates to help with the food drive.

Let everybody know about it. Make posters advertising your local food drive. Ask local businesses and places of worship to let you hang your posters. Ask the newspaper to run an article. Choosing a local or neighborhood newspaper is more likely to bring results than, say, calling the *New York Times*.

Collect the food. Ask if you can put food baskets in local grocery stores or places of prayer.

Deliver the food. Find someone with a vehicle to haul the food donations to the food bank.

At the end, put up posters to thank people for their donations and write news articles to report how well the community responded.

Letter Writing Campaign for Prisoners of Conscience

Civil rights workers filled southern jails in 1964. Jail was never fun or easy. Jail was part of the price of freedom. They went to jail for their beliefs. They were prisoners of conscience.

Today prisoners of conscience still sit in jails. Amnesty International keeps records of their cases. They ask people to send letters for prisoners of conscience. The letters go to government officials around the world. Sometimes the letters ask for protection: "I want you to keep this person safe from torture and abuse." Sometimes the letters ask for freedom: "I believe this person should be released from jail."

The letters let government officials know that someone is watching, that someone cares for the prisoner of conscience in their jail. Often the letters keep prisoners safe from abuse. Sometimes letters even save lives.

You can be part of Amnesty's letter-writing campaign. Find Amnesty International on-line at www.amnesty-usa.org/ or write to Amnesty International at Midwest Regional Office, 53 W. Jackson, Room 731, Chicago, IL 60604. The telephone number for this office is (312) 427-2060.

Freedom Feast

Freedom Summer volunteers ate new foods common in the South. Young, white northern students tasted gumbo, sweet potato pie, fried catfish, hush puppies, biscuits and gravy, grits, collard greens, red beans and rice, ham hocks, and black-eyed peas.

Eating with someone meant being their friend. Eating with a family meant sharing their life. Preparing food was an act of love. People took pride in cooking good food. Poor people took pride in sharing what little they had.

Today you can find many of these foods in the frozen food sections of grocery stores all over the country. You could taste the foods of Freedom Summer by microwaving a box of frozen food. That's not how Freedom Summer worked, though!

If you want a real taste of Freedom Summer, a real Freedom Feast, you have to cook. You can't cook for just one person—you have to feed friends. So here are some recipes for traditional southern foods. You can start with these and add your own favorites.

You can have your feast at home, or invite a speaker and serve your feast in a church basement or sell tickets to your feast and donate the money to a civil rights organization.

Gumbo

6 servings

Ingredients

5 tablespoons vegetable oil

1 pound of sliced okra (can be fresh, canned, or frozen)

2 large onions, chopped

3 celery ribs, chopped

4 cups water

1 or 2 pounds of chicken (could be wings, thighs, drumsticks, or cut up chicken breasts)

1 pound of sausage (kielbasa or spicy Italian sausage taste good)

1/4 cup flour

Salt

Freshly ground black pepper

Cayenne pepper (more or less, depending on how spicy you like your gumbo)

2 tablespoons filé powder

Utensils

Cast-iron pot

Measuring spoons

Wooden spoon

Cutting board

Knife

Frying pan

Wire whisk

Measuring cup

Directions

In a large cast-iron pot, heat 2 tablespoons of oil. Sauté the okra for 15 minutes, stirring constantly. Add the onions and celery and cook for another 5 minutes. Add 4 cups of water and simmer for 15 minutes.

In a large frying pan, heat the other 3 tablespoons of oil. Brown the chicken and the sausage. Cut the sausage into 1-inch pieces. If you use chicken breasts, cut them up, too. Add the chicken and sausage pieces to the okra mixture.

Stir the flour into the fat remaining in the frying pan. Cook over medium heat, stirring constantly, for 15-20 minutes. When the flour and fat turn into a thick, nut-brown mixture, remove from heat.

Using a wire whisk, mix about 1 cup of the okra liquid into the frying pan. When this is well mixed, pour it all into the large kettle.

Turn the heat on high and stir constantly until the gumbo boils. Then lower the heat and simmer for at least half an hour.

Season with salt, black pepper, and cayenne pepper to taste. Stir in the filé powder 5 minutes before serving. Enjoy!

Corn Bread

12 servings

Ingredients

1 cup flour

1 cup cornmeal

2 teaspoons baking powder

$\frac{1}{2}$ teaspoon salt

1 egg, beaten

$\frac{1}{2}$ cup honey

1 cup milk

$\frac{1}{4}$ cup vegetable oil

Utensils

8-inch square pan or 12-cup muffin pan

2 bowls

Measuring spoons

Measuring cups

Fork

Mixing spoon

Directions

Heat the oven to 400°. Grease an 8-inch square pan or 12-cup muffin pan. Mix the flour, corn-meal, baking powder, and salt in one bowl. With a fork, beat the egg in another bowl and add the honey, milk, and vegetable oil. Combine dry and wet ingredients, stirring just until they are mixed. Pour into the greased pan or muffin cups.

Bake for 20–25 minutes (pan) or 15–20 minutes (muffins). The corn bread is done when the top is golden brown and a wooden toothpick inserted in the middle comes out clean. Serve warm, with honey and butter.

The Struggle
Continues

Late 1960s,

Keeping On

The Struggle Continues

Introduction

Although southern states resisted following the legal directions of the 1964 Civil Rights Act and the 1965 Voting Rights Act, the laws gave new tools and new hope to the Civil Rights Movement. In the middle of the 1960s the combined impact of new laws, a new movement toward black pride and black power, and the escalating war in Vietnam transformed the movement. [Note: The text of both of these Acts can be found at the back of this book.]

Black Power

On June 4, 1966, James Meredith set out on a 220-mile march from Memphis, Tennessee, to Jackson, Mississippi. Meredith was well known as the first black man to enter the University of Mississippi in 1962, over the violent resistance of the university and the state of Mississippi. When he crossed the Mississippi state line, he was shot down.

As Meredith was rushed to the hospital, leaders of all the civil rights organizations gathered in Memphis to decide how to continue his march. Through the nights, leaders of SNCC, CORE, SCLC, and the NAACP debated strategy and policy. The strongest voice belonged to a SNCC leader, Stokely Carmichael. As the large group continued the march, Stokely spoke a new message to people along the way:

> *Don't be afraid. Don't be ashamed. We want black power. We want black power. We want black power. We want black power. We want black power. That's right. That's what we want, black power. And we don't have to be ashamed of it.*
>
> *We have stayed here and we've begged the President, we've begged the federal government. That's all we've been doing, begging, begging. It's time we stand up and take over. Take over.*

As the march neared Jackson, Mississippi, it was attacked by police using tear gas and billy clubs. President Lyndon Johnson refused to send federal troops to protect the marchers. They continued, led now by James Meredith, who had been released from the hospital. Meredith reiterated the purpose of his march: to challenge the fear that supported white domination of black people.

Reclaiming Identity

In recognition of his African heritage, Stokely Carmichael later changed his name to Kwame Ture.

Stokely's Message of Black Power

Stokely Carmichael repeated his message, and eager crowds answered:

Now from now on when they ask you what you want, you know what to
tell them. What do you want?

Black power!

What do you want?

Black power!

What do you want?

Black power!

Everybody, what do you want?

Black power!

That's what we gon' get.

The leaders of the other civil rights groups were appalled by Carmichael's message. They feared that it would alienate white support and erode the foundations of nonviolence on which the movement had been built.

Many white people across the country were outraged or frightened by talk of black pride and black power. Some felt betrayed—they wanted to believe that there were no differences between black and white people, and they could

not accept pride in blackness. Others were afraid that talk of black power would mean the end of nonviolence. And some were disillusioned because they had seen themselves as gracious white benefactors to poor, powerless black people. Those white people who remained committed to the Civil Rights Movement struggled to identify their own racism and to understand the new ideas of black pride and power.

War and the Death of a Dreamer

At the same time that black power emerged, college campuses across the country found a new cause for concern. The United States' involvement in the war in Vietnam was escalating. More and more young men were being drafted to fight and die half a world away. To many, it looked as if they were fighting and dying for no good reason.

Young people committed to social change believed in both civil rights and the anti-war movement. They wanted change in foreign policy, an end to discrimination, an end to poverty and hunger, and more freedom for themselves on their college campuses. The Civil Rights

Movement, the anti-war movement, and the youth movement all claimed the energies of people committed to social change.

Dr. Martin Luther King, Jr. wrestled with the problem of the Vietnam War. As a person committed to nonviolence, he could not support war. Moreover, he saw this war as a war by white America against people of color in Asia. Though many advised him to "stick to civil rights," his conscience compelled King to speak out against the war.

He drew connections between the war in Vietnam and poverty at home:

> We are spending all of this money for death and destruction, and not nearly enough money for life and constructive development . . . when the guns of war become a national obsession, social needs inevitably suffer.

In 1968 King worked on plans for a Poor People's Encampment in Washington. This protest against poverty would bring together people of all races in a common cause: ending poverty in the richest nation on earth.

Newsday, Inc. ©1965

The Reverend Martin Luther King, Jr. addresses a rally in Lakeview, New York, in 1965.

As always, King's time was claimed by many groups. When garbage workers in Memphis, Tennessee, went on strike for higher wages to

Though many advised him to "stick to civil rights," his conscience compelled King to speak out against the war.

The Poor People's Campaign of Nassau County presented the Reverend Martin Luther King, Jr., who is addressing a packed school auditorium at Southside High School, Rockville Center, Melville, New York, in 1968.

support their families, they called for his help. King went to Memphis to march alongside the garbage workers. He was assassinated there on April 4, 1968.

The assassination of Dr. King shocked the entire world. In the United States the anger and despair of black communities erupted into violence in many cities.

In Chicago, most black people hid inside their homes. Saddened and fearful, they listened to shouts and gunfire outside. In the streets, other black people tore down the bars on the windows of stores in their neighborhoods. They ransacked stores and then set fires. Police and firefighters, all white, could not control the situation. The governor ordered the National Guard into Chicago.

White neighborhoods were largely unaffected by the violence. Black neighborhoods looked like war zones. With stores gutted by fires and streets littered with debris, the helmeted National Guard looked like an occupying army. Never were the lines of segregation between black and white Chicago more clearly drawn.

The Movement Moves North

By 1968 the Civil Rights Movement was active in northern cities, including Chicago.

Cicero is a suburb of Chicago. In 1966 Cicero was all white, kept that way not by law but by the people who lived there. Residents, real estate agents, and bankers cooperated to keep Cicero white. Real estate agents did not show homes in Cicero to black families. Home-owners sold only to other white people. Bankers restricted loans to white people.

If an African American family bought a house, they faced danger. In Cicero and in other white neighborhoods, they faced bombs and beatings.

Dr. Martin Luther King, Jr. had led a march in Cicero in 1966, asking for an end to segregation there. His march was met with jeers and hatred. White people spat on marchers. They threw rocks. Dr. King was hit by a rock and some other marchers were hurt.

The outbreak of hatred in Cicero shocked the nation. Others learned what African Americans already knew. Racism was a fact of life throughout the country. Prejudice and segregation were not southern problems. They were (and are) American problems.

Operation Breadbasket

Realizing that segregation has economic effects, the SCLC founded Operation Breadbasket. Operation Breadbasket organized around economic issues, like trying to convince business

Coretta Scott King Becomes a Leader

Coretta Scott King was at home in Atlanta, Georgia, on April 4, 1968, when her husband was shot in Memphis. Four days later she went to Memphis with three of their four children. On April 8, she led the march that Martin had organized. King's funeral was held the next day.

Two months later, she spoke at the Poor People's Campaign in Washington. With her husband a martyr to the movement, King became a leader in seeking peace and justice. She founded and led the Martin Luther King, Jr. Center for Social Change. In 1995, their youngest son, Dexter Scott King, took over the leadership of the Center.

people that hiring black employees made good economic sense.

Breadbasket organizers showed businesses how many black customers they had. If a business hired black employees, it would gain black customers. If a business treated black customers well, it would make more money. Sometimes employers listened. Sometimes they did not. Segregation and prejudice remain all-American problems.

Reverend Jesse Jackson marched with Dr. King in the South. Then he moved to Chicago, where he headed Operation Breadbasket.

Jackson was born to a teenage mother in 1941 in South Carolina. His mother worked as a maid for whites. She was not married to his father, Noah Robinson, so Jesse began life as Jesse Louis Burns. He was raised by his mother and grandmother. When Burns was just three years old, his mother married Charles Jackson. For years, the child lived away from his mother. He and his grandmother lived nearby, in a run-down home.

Other children taunted him. "Jesse ain't got no daddy," they called. "Your daddy ain't none of your daddy. You ain't nothing but a nobody." Burns felt their taunts deeply. When Jesse was thirteen, Charles Jackson adopted him. He gave Jesse his name. Jesse Burns became Jesse Jackson.

Jackson got his first job at the age of six, helping relatives deliver wood. As he grew older, he kept on working. He caddied at a golf course. He waited tables at an airport restaurant. He worked as a carhop at a drive-in restaurant.

In high school, Jackson starred on baseball and football teams. He won a football scholarship to an Illinois university. After a year, he returned south. He enrolled in North Carolina A & T State University. There he met Jacqueline Lavinia Brown. She was a smart, tough, beautiful young woman. Like Jackson, she had been born into poverty. She was the daughter of migrant workers and had been raised by an aunt. Jesse and Jackie fell in love and married.

Although he took time out from college for demonstrations and jail, Jackson graduated in 1964 and entered the Chicago Theological Seminary.

In March 1965, Jackson watched Selma's Bloody Sunday on television. He felt he could not remain safely distant from the battle. Joining thousands of others in Selma, he met Dr. King. A year later, Dr. King made Jackson the Chicago head of Operation Breadbasket. A year after that, he became the national head of Operation Breadbasket. He was only 25 years old.

In Chicago Reverend Jackson held mass meetings every Saturday morning. He preached a message of self-respect, as he led people in a chanted litany:

I AM SOMEBODY!
RESPECT ME . . .
NEVER NEGLECT ME . . .

I AM SOMEBODY!
I WANT TO LEARN
'CAUSE MY MIND IS A PEARL
I CAN DO ANYTHING
IN THE WHOLE WORLD!
I AM SOMEBODY!

Operation Breadbasket demanded better schools for black children and jobs for black men and women. Breadbasket worked through organizing, marching, preaching, and teaching. Jackson focused attention on the plight of black people and of all poor people. Operation Breadbasket emphasized the common interests of poor people of all colors.

Operation Breadbasket members visited grocery stores and compared stores and prices in black and white neighborhoods. They found stores in black neighborhoods charging higher prices, while stores in white neighborhoods often had better food and lower prices.

Sometimes Breadbasket members found filthy conditions in stores. At one store, Operation Breadbasket members discovered frozen mud and blood on the bottom of the walk-in meat cooler. They picketed the store, demanding that the store clean up its premises. They said clean stores showed respect for customers. Operation Breadbasket also marched outside large chain grocery stores, demanding that good stores locate in black neighborhoods and hire black people.

On April 4, 1968, Jackson went with Dr. King to Memphis. He marched along with Dr. King. He was there when Dr. King was shot.

In 1971 Jackson resigned from the SCLC. He founded a new organization—PUSH. PUSH stands for People United to Save Humanity. Later he moved from Operation PUSH to the Rainbow Coalition. With each step, his following increased. He became the best-known African American leader in the country. The next step seemed logical. He would run for president.

In 1984 and again in 1988 Jesse Jackson ran for president. People of all colors backed Jesse Jackson. He won delegates from all-black neighborhoods in big cities. He won delegates from all-white farm communities in the Midwest. Although he did not win the Democratic presidential nomination, Jackson's candidacy united many people in the struggle for equal rights for all.

Operation Breadbasket demanded better schools for black children and jobs for black men and women.

Congressman Jesse Jackson, Jr.

Jesse Jackson, Jr. was born in 1965, while his father was in Alabama marching from Selma to Montgomery. As a child, he marched along with his father. He attended Chicago public schools. Then, like his father, he went to college at North Carolina A & T State University. After college he went to seminary, and then to law school.

Politics was part of young Jesse's whole life. At the age of 30, he won his first election to Congress representing the second district in Illinois. In 1996 he was re-elected with 94 percent of the vote! He represents a district with many poor people. Black and white, they know Jesse Jackson, Jr. will help them all he can.

Though laws forbid segregation and discrimination, both still exist.

Though he did not win, he changed the face of politics in the United States. In the following years, he often represented the United States abroad. He won the release of a U.S. pilot in Syria in 1983. In 1991 he won the release of hundreds of foreign prisoners in Kuwait. In 1999 he negotiated the release of U.S. soldiers held in Serbia.

Jesse Jackson and his son led a Rainbow Coalition march in Georgia in 1995. Together they preached and led the call and response from marchers:

Save our children—keep hope alive!
Help our seniors—keep hope alive!
No more violence—keep hope alive!
Affirmative action—keep hope alive!

Reverend John Gibbons marched with the Jacksons. Later, he told his congregation: "Jesse Jackson keeps hope alive for many of the poorest of the poor."

Continuing Challenges

Many people feared that the Civil Rights Movement would die with Martin Luther King, Jr.'s death. It did not. The Civil Rights Movement lives on today. Some things have changed. In the 1950s and 1960s laws ordered segregation. Today laws require integration. Today stores, buses, and lunch counters are integrated.

Though laws forbid segregation and discrimination, both still exist. Today many groups that grew out of the Civil Rights Movement of the 1960s continue to challenge discrimination wherever it appears.

Express Yourself!

Buttons, like the one worn by the demonstrator pictured in chapter 8, have been used to express political opinions for more than a century. Political buttons were especially popular during the 1960s.

You can make and wear a button to express your commitments. Or you can rent a button-making machine and outfit your whole class, club, or organization!

Materials

Drawing paper

Pencils

Markers

Paint

Self-laminating pages

Safety pins

Button backs (optional)

Directions

Use your imagination and artistic ability to design your buttons. What cause do you want to support? What opinion do you want to express? Think of a symbol or slogan to convey your message. Here are some examples to spark your imagination.

Symbols

- A black fist was used in the 1960s as a symbol of black power
- A dove symbolizes peace
- A rainbow is often used as a symbol of gay pride

Slogans

- Freedom Now
- We Shall Overcome
- Black Is Beautiful
- I Am Somebody!
- All Children of One God
- Sisterhood Is Powerful
- Keep Hope Alive
- Flower Power
- Make Love, Not War
- Peace with Justice

Draw, paint, or use the computer to make your design. Keep in mind that words or symbols should contrast with the background, so that they are easily visible. You can make your design just the right size for your button, or you can make it larger and then use a photocopier to reduce its size.

After you have the design, you need to turn it into a wearable button. The simplest and least expensive way to do this is to mount your design on tagboard or heavy paper. Then cover it with clear, self-adhering laminate. Tape a small safety pin to the back and wear it with pride!

For slightly fancier buttons, visit a sewing or craft store. You can buy various blank buttons on which to mount your own design.

If you want to make a large number of buttons, you can rent a button-making machine from a novelty shop. Look in the yellow pages under "Novelties."

Tie-Dye Delight

One of the distinctive clothing styles popular among the young hippies of the 1960s was tie-dyed clothing. Now you can make your own tie-dyed T-shirt.

Materials

White cotton T-shirt
Rubber bands
Fabric dye in 1 or more colors
Rubber gloves

Directions

Before it is dyed, the T-shirt must be washed to remove anything that could interfere with the colors. (Sometimes something called "sizing" is added to fabric during the manufacturing process. This must be washed out, even if it is not visible, before tie-dyeing.) After washing, dry the T-shirt completely.

Twist the T-shirt into various designs. You might scrunch up the sleeves and secure them with a rubber band. You might fold the T-shirt like an accordion, and then use rubber bands to scrunch it together in various places.

Read through the directions on the dye package carefully. Do you need to use hot water or cold? Many, but not all, dyes will require hot water. Prepare a place where you can use the dye without damaging furniture or other clothing. This needs to be a large enough place so you can pour dye over the T-shirt.

After you have prepared the dye, put on your rubber gloves. Carefully pour the dye over the parts of the T-shirt. The T-shirt should be wet, but not completely saturated. You want the different parts to have different color patterns as they dry.

Let the T-shirt air-dry completely. When it is dry, take off the rubber bands and unfold it. Now you have a beautiful, original work of art to wear! To preserve the colors, and to protect other clothing, carefully follow the directions on the dye package for washing and drying your T-shirt. The first few times you wash it, wash it separately from other clothing.

10

Keep Hope Alive

Civil Rights

Today

Keep Hope Alive

149

Despite laws forbidding discrimination in housing, many neighborhoods remain mostly segregated by color or ethnicity.

Introduction

Today we stand at the beginning of the twenty-first century. Looking back, we know that we have come a long way. Laws prohibit segregation in public places. All citizens have a right to vote. African Americans serve in Congress. They serve on the Supreme Court. The birthday of Martin Luther King, Jr. is a national holiday.

Yet we still have far to go. Most people still live in neighborhoods segregated by race and by income level. Schools struggle to maintain some kind of integration. Often they fail. On average, African Americans earn less money than white Americans. On average, women earn less money than men. In a country brimming with wealth, one-quarter of all children still live in poverty.

De Facto Segregation

In the 1950s and 1960s much segregation was *de jure*, meaning "by law." Today, most segregation is called *de facto*, meaning "in fact."

The Civil Rights Act of 1964 (pages 159–172) broke down many legal barriers. The Voting

Continuing Inequality

According to a 1999 U.S. Census Bureau report, an African American man with a college education earns on average $13,000 less than a white man with a college education. The median family income for African American families in 1997 was $28,600, compared to a median white family income of $49,640.

Rights Act of 1965 (pages 173–176) protected everyone's right to vote. De jure segregation is gone. De facto segregation remains.

Despite laws forbidding discrimination in housing, many neighborhoods remain mostly segregated by color or ethnicity. Some of this segregation is due to discrimination. Sometimes banks give mortgages to white people more easily than to African Americans. Some real estate agents encourage African Americans to buy in segregated neighborhoods. They try not to show homes in traditionally white neighborhoods to African American home buyers.

Sometimes housing discrimination is violent. Even at the beginning of the twenty-first century, the Ku Klux Klan exists. An African American family moving into an all-white neighborhood in some cities may meet with violence. Rocks or bricks break windows. A cross burns in front of the house. Children are harassed.

When neighborhoods are segregated, schools remain segregated. In many large cities schools are mostly African American, Hispanic American, and Asian American. In nearby suburbs schools are mostly white.

Discrimination in employment is illegal. But it is also hard to prove. In many places discrimination continues. Some employers try not to hire African Americans. They find reasons to reject job applications from African Americans. They choose white applicants over African American applicants.

Some jobs are filled by word of mouth. A job opens up. A worker tells her cousin about it. Her cousin applies and is hired. When most workers are white, they usually tell other white people. Only white people hear about the jobs. More white people are hired.

Sometimes an African American person faces coldness every day on the job. He or she meets daily snubs from other workers. Managers make

---

School Segregation Continues

According to a Howard University study, African American students are still in largely segregated schools, partly because of "the out-migration of whites from urban to suburban school districts and the ineffective implementation of court orders designed to increase school integration in the late 1960s and 1970s."

---

it clear that prospects for promotion are slim. The work atmosphere discourages integration.

Civil Rights Work Today

Today's Civil Rights Movement takes many forms. African Americans work for justice and equality. Feminists work for equal rights for women. Mexican Americans and Asian Americans demand inclusion and recognition. Gay, lesbian, bisexual, and transgendered people insist on dignity and equality.

Organizations are formed to work on problems that become apparent in different times and places. For example, in Mississippi in the 1960s SNCC tackled the problem of gaining access to voting. One of the leaders in that effort was Bob Moses. In the 1980s Moses began the Algebra Project. His story illustrates the changing ways in which people work for civil rights.

From Voting to Algebra

Robert Moses grew up in New York and began college at Harvard University. If any young African American man was poised for success, that man was Bob Moses. Then he left it all behind him. Moses dropped out of Harvard University. A child of the North, he headed to the Deep South to put his body on the line, joining with other young people to form SNCC.

Moses was both a charismatic leader and a humble man who believed deeply in sharing power. Although Moses tried to stay out of the spotlight, friends and followers always wanted to hear what he thought.

In 1965 Moses left SNCC and wandered through the country, begging religious leaders to unite against the Vietnam War. They told him not to speak out on the evil of war. By speaking out, they said, African Americans would risk everything they had gained. Moses believed the war was unjust and immoral and he would not be silenced.

At 31 years old, Moses was too old for the draft. In spite of this he received a draft notice in 1966. He fled to Canada and later to Africa. In Tanzania he married Janet Jemmott, whom he had met when she was a SNCC worker during Freedom Summer.

They taught school together in a Tanzanian village for the next 10 years. Then they returned to the United States with their four children. In the 1980s Moses started a new kind of Freedom School.

Moses was now a math teacher. He said that learning first-year algebra was as important as having the right to vote, and he founded the Algebra Project. Today the Algebra Project still helps students of color and poor students to learn algebra. Thanks to Bob Moses, they will have a better educational start in the world.

Just as he did in the 1960s, Moses encourages other people to become leaders. "Leadership is there in the people," he says. "You don't have to worry about that. . . . If you go out and work with your people, then the leadership will emerge. . . . We don't know who they are now; we don't need to know. But the leadership will emerge from the movement that emerges."

Fighting for the Future

As Moses points out, legal rights are not enough. People also need the skills to use their rights, to hold jobs, to make their way in the world. One of the enduring legacies of discrimination against people of color is poverty. African Americans, Hispanic Americans, and many immi-

A Freedom Summer Reunion Message

Returning to Mississippi for a Freedom Summer reunion in 1994, former SNCC coordinator Elizabeth Martinez made the following observation.

We need a new Civil Rights Movement. Call it human rights if you prefer, but we still live in a time when the denial of civil rights becomes the denial of humanity. Look at the beating of Rodney King, the repeated lynchings of blacks in Mississippi jails, so many current examples. Look at the forces seeking to deny health care and schooling to Latino and other immigrant children because they lack the right piece of paper. We need to fight all such barbarity with a movement that calls upon all colors.

grant groups suffer higher rates of poverty than white Americans. Their children may continue the cycle of poverty, or break out of it. Marian Wright Edelman is one of many people whose commitment to civil rights led them to focus on ways to help families break the cycle of poverty.

Marian Wright was born in South Carolina in 1939. She was the youngest of five children. Her father, Arthur Wright, was a minister. Her mother, Maggie Bowen Wright, was an activist, who also ran a home for the elderly.

Marian Wright Edelman and CDF gave the poor a voice in Washington.

The Inequality of Poverty

In 1996, 7.4 million Americans lived in poverty. Ten of every one hundred African Americans and Hispanic Americans lived in poverty, compared to only five of every one hundred white Americans.

Wright's parents expected much of their children. They wanted their children to get good educations. Education was only the beginning. "Working for the community," Edelman recalled later, "was as much a part of our existence as eating and sleeping and church."

Wright went to Spelman College and then won a scholarship to study in Europe. She attended the Sorbonne in Paris, and also studied in Switzerland and Russia.

When Wright returned home in 1959, she felt a huge culture shock. In Europe people treated her as a human being. In the American South they treated her as less than human. Wright quickly joined the Civil Rights Movement.

After attending Yale University Law School on a scholarship, she went back to the South.

She used her legal training to work for both SNCC and the NAACP. Sometimes she went to jail along with her clients. At the age of 25 she headed the NAACP Legal Defense Fund. She also became the first African American woman lawyer in Mississippi.

In 1968 Wright moved to Washington, D.C. She married Peter Edelman. She first met Edelman in Mississippi. He was a white civil rights worker there. Both Marian and Peter continued to work for civil rights. They had three children.

In 1973 Marian Wright Edelman founded the Children's Defense Fund (CDF). Twenty years later, she reflected on the beginning of the CDF. "It became clear to me that the poor needed a voice in Washington, just like General Motors and other big interests," she said. Marian Wright Edelman and CDF gave the poor a voice in Washington.

Teenage pregnancy was the first target of CDF. CDF put messages on posters and radio ads. They urged teens to wait before becoming pregnant. Edelman saw teen pregnancy as "ensur[ing] black child poverty for the next generation."

CDF helped pass the Act for Better Child

Care in 1987. CDF urges people to prevent problems, instead of waiting until children have problems to act. Education and youth employment are among the concerns of CDF. CDF is still a lobbyist and a strong voice for poor children.

Marian Wright Edelman has written several books and has taught at Harvard University. Throughout her life, she has continued "working for the community," as her parents taught her.

Making a Difference

Activism today takes many forms. Barbara Jordan worked for civil rights during the exciting years of the 1960s. Then she turned to different arenas to continue to work for the greater good of all people. She continued her work for civil rights as a politician and as a teacher.

Barbara Charline Jordan was born in 1936 in Houston, Texas. "We were poor," she later recalled, "but so was everyone else around us, so we didn't notice it." Her father was a Baptist minister. Religion and church remained important throughout her life.

In those segregated years Jordan attended an African American high school and an African

The Influence of Race

Peter Edelman, writing in the *New York Times* in 1999, observed that:

Too many jobs pay poorly, often because they are only part-time. Moreover, two million people work full-time all year and can't get their families out of poverty. More than 70 percent of poor children live in families where somebody has income from work. Lousy pay from work is the biggest source of poverty for people who aren't elderly.

And all of these problems hit minorities the hardest. We should remember that race is an underlying issue in the debate on poverty.

American college, Texas Southern University. She was a member of the debate team at TSU. Her debate team was the first from an African American university to compete in an annual tournament at Baylor College. She won first place in junior oratory at that contest.

Jordan studied law at Boston University. Few African Americans, and even fewer women, attended law school in 1959, but Jordan did not let that stop her. She was ready to be "the first" over and over again.

Barbara Jordan was the first African American woman from the South to serve in the U.S. Congress.

Children's Freedom Schools

The Children's Defense Fund also coordinates Freedom Schools with the Black Community Crusade for Children. These schools enroll children ages 5 to 18 for 6-week summer sessions.

Jordan became the first African American woman to serve in the Texas Senate. Years later, at her funeral, a friend recalled her struggles there. "In the Legislature, she endured comments directed to 'that black washerwoman.' We don't remember the people who made those remarks," the friend said. "We remember Barbara Jordan."

Jordan left the Texas Senate in 1973, moving up to the U.S. House of Representatives. Once again, Jordan marked a first, becoming the first African American woman from the South to serve in the U.S. Congress. Over and over during her three terms, she appealed to the conscience of the Congress. "What the people want is very simple," she said. "They want an America as good as its promise."

In 1976 Jordan was first again as the first African American woman to give a keynote speech at a national political convention. Jordan spoke to the Democratic national convention with the same skill that had won the college contest. At the end of her speech, people stood and cheered. Over and over, they chanted, "We want Barbara!"

Jordan left Congress in 1979. She had enjoyed her years there, but now she wanted to teach young people. "I have faith in young people," she said, "because I know the strongest emotions which prevail are those of love and caring and belief and tolerance."

Jordan's students at the University of Texas loved her. They called her a hero, an example, an inspiration. She taught public policy and ethics in government. Her example, some students said, made it possible to believe that public service could still be a noble calling.

Besides teaching, she wrote and spoke about the rights and needs of the poor and of children. She continued to speak for civil rights. "One

Children rest from picket line duty in 1962 at Malverne High School on Long Island in New York.

Young people and

children made the

Civil Rights

Movement of the

1960s a success.

thing is clear to me," she wrote. "We, as human beings, must be willing to accept people who are different from ourselves."

For years Jordan suffered from multiple sclerosis. In her last years, she had to use a wheelchair. Then she got leukemia. She died in 1996. Students, friends, politicians, and even the President of the United States came to her funeral.

One of her students said that Barbara Jordan "made it possible to think you could make a difference." She certainly made a difference in Texas and in the world.

Passing the Torch

Julian Bond worked in the Civil Rights Movement as a member of SNCC. Later, he held political office and taught at universities. In a speech later reprinted in *The Black Collegian*, he called young people's activism:

> . . . a sign of hope and optimism. They give reassurance that seriousness and commitment can be transmitted through generations, that torches can be passed. . . .

Racial Progress in Congress

In 1966, there were just six African American members of the United States Congress. In 1999, there were 39.

Sadly—or luckily—for those who yearn to do their part, there are plenty of torches to go around.

Young people and children made the Civil Rights Movement of the 1960s a success. Their protests and sacrifices toppled an entire social and legal system of segregation. Today many of their children continue to work for human rights for all.

At the beginning of the twenty-first century, we see many problems. Each problem presents a challenge. Today's children and young people will meet those challenges. There is still exciting work for all of us to do.

Title VII of the Civil Rights Act of 1964

Note   The following is the text of Title VII of the Civil Rights Act of 1964 (Pub. L. 88-352) (Title VII), as amended, as it appears in volume 42 of the United States Code, beginning at section 2000e. Title VII prohibits employment discrimination based on race, color, religion, sex, and national origin. The Civil Rights Act of 1991 (Pub. L. 102-166) (CRA) amends several sections of Title VII. These amendments appear in boldface type. In addition, section 102 of the Civil Rights Act amends the Revised Statutes by adding a new section following section 1977 (42 U.S.C. 1981), to provide for the recovery of compensatory and punitive damages in cases of intentional violations of Title VII, the Americans with Disabilities Act of 1990, and section 501 of the Rehabilitation Act of 1973.

An Act

To enforce the constitutional right to vote, to confer jurisdiction upon the district courts of the United States to provide injunctive relief against discrimination in public accommodations, to authorize the Attorney General to institute suits to protect constitutional rights in public facilities and public education, to extend the Commission on Civil Rights, to prevent discrimination in federally assisted programs, to establish a Commission on Equal Employment Opportunity, and for other purposes.

Be it enacted by the Senate and House of Representatives of the United States of America in Congress assembled, That this Act may be cited as the "Civil Rights Act of 1964."

DEFINITIONS

SEC. 2000e. [Section 701]

For the purposes of this subchapter—

(a) The term "person" includes one or more individuals, governments, governmental agencies, political subdivisions, labor unions, partnerships, associations, corporations, legal representatives, mutual companies, joint-stock companies, trusts, unincorporated organizations, trustees, trustees in cases under title 11 [bankruptcy], or receivers.

(b) The term "employer" means a person engaged in an industry affecting commerce who has fifteen or more employees for each working day in each of twenty or more calendar weeks in the current or preceding calendar year, and any agent of such a person, but such term does not include (1) the United States, a corporation wholly owned by the Government of the United States, an Indian tribe, or any department or agency of the District of Columbia subject by statute to procedures of the competitive service (as defined in section 2102 of title 5 [of the United States Code]), or (2) a bona fide private membership club (other than a labor organization) which is exempt from taxation under section 501(c) of title 26 [the Internal Revenue Code of 1954], except that during the first year after March 24, 1972 [the date of enactment of the Equal Employment Opportunity Act of 1972], persons having fewer than twenty-five employees (and their agents) shall not be considered employers.

(c) The term "employment agency" means any person regularly undertaking with or without compensation to procure employees for an employer or to procure for employees opportunities to work for an employer and includes an agent of such a person.

(d) The term "labor organization" means a labor organization engaged in an industry affecting commerce, and any agent of such an organization, and includes any organization of any kind, any agency, or employee representation committee, group, association, or plan so engaged in which employees participate and which exists for the purpose, in whole or in part, of dealing with employers concerning grievances, labor disputes, wages, rates of pay, hours, or other terms or conditions of employment, and any conference, general committee, joint or system board, or joint council so engaged which is subordinate to a national or international labor organization.

(e) A labor organization shall be deemed to be engaged in an industry affecting commerce if (1) it maintains or operates a hiring hall or hiring office which procures employees for an employer or procures for employees opportunities to work for an employer, or (2) the number of its members (or, where it is a labor organization composed of other labor organizations or their representatives, if the aggregate number of the members of such other labor organization) is (A) twenty-five or more during the first year after March 24, 1972 [the date of enactment of the Equal Employment Opportunity Act of 1972], or (B) fifteen or more thereafter, and such labor organization—

(1) is the certified representative of employees under the provisions of the National Labor Relations Act, as amended [29 U.S.C. 151 et seq.], or the Railway Labor Act, as amended [45 U.S.C. 151 et seq.];

(2) although not certified, is a national or international labor organization or a local labor organization recognized or acting as the representative of employees of an employer or employers engaged in an industry affecting commerce; or

(3) has chartered a local labor organization or subsidiary body which is representing or actively seeking to represent employees of employers within the meaning of paragraph (1) or (2); or

(4) has been chartered by a labor organization representing or actively seeking to represent employees within the meaning of paragraph (1) or (2) as the local or subordinate body through which such employees may enjoy membership or become affiliated with such labor organization; or

(5) is a conference, general committee, joint or system board, or joint council subordinate to a national or international labor organization, which includes a labor organization engaged in an industry affecting commerce within the meaning of any of the preceding paragraphs of this subsection.

(f) The term "employee" means an individual employed by an employer, except that the term "employee" shall not include any person elected to public office in any State or political subdivision of any State by the qualified voters thereof, or any person chosen by such officer to be on such officer's personal staff, or an appointee on the policy making level or an immediate adviser with respect to the exercise of the constitutional or legal powers of the office. The exemption set forth in the preceding sentence shall not include employees subject to the civil service laws of a State government, governmental agency or political subdivision. With respect to employment in a foreign country, such term includes an individual who is a citizen of the United States.

(g) The term "commerce" means trade, traffic, commerce, transportation, transmission, or communication among the several States; or between a State and any place outside thereof; or within the District of Columbia, or a possession of the United States; or between points in the same State but through a point outside thereof.

(h) The term "industry affecting commerce" means any activity, business, or industry in commerce or in which a labor dispute would hinder or obstruct commerce or the free flow of commerce and includes any activity or industry "affecting commerce" within the meaning of the Labor-Management Reporting and Disclosure Act of 1959 [29 U.S.C. 401 et seq.], and further includes any governmental industry, business, or activity.

(i) The term "State" includes a State of the United States, the District of Columbia, Puerto Rico, the Virgin Islands, American Samoa, Guam, Wake Island, the Canal Zone, and Outer Continental Shelf lands defined in the Outer Continental Shelf Lands Act [43 U.S.C. 1331 et seq.].

(j) The term "religion" includes all aspects of religious observance and practice, as well as belief, unless an employer demonstrates that he is unable to reasonably accommodate to an employee's or prospective employee's religious observance or practice without undue hardship on the conduct of the employer's business.

(k) The terms "because of sex" or "on the basis of sex" include, but are not limited to, because of or on the basis of pregnancy, childbirth, or related medical conditions; and women affected by pregnancy, childbirth, or related medical conditions shall be treated the same for all employment-related purposes, including receipt of benefits under fringe benefit programs, as other persons not so affected but similar in their ability or inability to work, and nothing in section 2000e-2(h) of this title [section 703(h)] shall be interpreted to permit otherwise. This subsection shall not require an employer to pay for health insurance benefits for abortion, except where the life of the mother would be endangered if the fetus were carried to term, or except where medical complications have arisen from an abortion: Provided, That nothing herein shall preclude an employer from providing abortion benefits or otherwise affect bargaining agreements in regard to abortion.

(l) The term "complaining party" means the Commission, the Attorney General, or a person who may bring an action or proceeding under this subchapter.

(m) The term "demonstrates" means meets the burdens of production and persuasion.

(n) The term "respondent" means an employer, employment agency, labor organization, joint labor-management committee controlling apprenticeship or other training or retraining program, including an on-the-job training program, or Federal entity subject to section 2000e-16 of this title.

EXEMPTION

SEC. 2000e-1. [Section 702]

(a) This subchapter shall not apply to an employer with respect to the employment of aliens outside any State, or to a religious corporation, association, educational institution, or society with respect to the employment of individuals of a particular religion to perform work connected with the carrying on by such corporation, association, educational institution, or society of its activities.

(b) It shall not be unlawful under section 2000e-2 or 2000e-3 of this title [section 703 or 704] for an employer (or a corporation controlled by an employer), labor organization, employment agency, or joint labor-management committee controlling apprenticeship or other training or retraining (including on-the-job training programs) to take any action otherwise prohibited by such section, with respect to an employee in a workplace in a foreign country if compliance with such section would cause such employer (or such corporation), such organization, such agency, or such committee to violate the law of the foreign country in which such workplace is located.

(c) (1) If an employer controls a corporation whose place of incorporation is a foreign country, any practice prohibited by section 2000e-2 or 2000e-3 of this title [section 703 or 704] engaged in by such corporation shall be presumed to be engaged in by such employer.

(2) Sections 2000e-2 and 2000e-3 of this title [sections 703 and 704] shall not apply with respect to the foreign operations of an employer that is a foreign person not controlled by an American employer.

(3) For purposes of this subsection, the determination of whether an employer controls a corporation shall be based on—

(A) the interrelation of operations;

(B) the common management;

(C) the centralized control of labor relations; and

(D) the common ownership or financial control, of the employer and the corporation.

UNLAWFUL EMPLOYMENT PRACTICES

SEC. 2000e-2. [Section 703]

(a) It shall be an unlawful employment practice for an employer—

(1) to fail or refuse to hire or to discharge any individual, or otherwise to discriminate against any individual with respect to his compensation, terms, conditions, or privileges of employment, because of such individual's race, color, religion, sex, or national origin; or

(2) to limit, segregate, or classify his employees or applicants for employment in any way which would deprive or tend to deprive any individual of employment opportunities or otherwise adversely affect his status as an employee, because of such individual's race, color, religion, sex, or national origin.

(b) It shall be an unlawful employment practice for an employment agency to fail or refuse to refer for employment, or otherwise to discriminate against, any individual because of his race, color, religion, sex, or national origin, or to classify or refer for employment any individual on the basis of his race, color, religion, sex, or national origin.

(c) It shall be an unlawful employment practice for a labor organization—

(1) to exclude or to expel from its membership, or otherwise to discriminate against, any individual because of his race, color, religion, sex, or national origin;

(2) to limit, segregate, or classify its membership or applicants for membership, or to classify or fail or refuse to refer for employment any individual, in any way which would deprive or tend to deprive any individual of employment opportunities, or would limit such employment opportunities or otherwise adversely affect his status as an employee or as an applicant for employment, because of such individual's race, color, religion, sex, or national origin; or

(3) to cause or attempt to cause an employer to discriminate against an individual in violation of this section.

(d) It shall be an unlawful employment practice for any employer, labor organization, or joint labor-management committee controlling apprenticeship or other training or retraining, including on-the-job training programs to discriminate against any individual because of his race, color, religion, sex, or national origin in admission to, or employment in, any program established to provide apprenticeship or other training.

(e) Notwithstanding any other provision of this subchapter,

(1) it shall not be an unlawful employment practice for an employer to hire and employ employees, for an employment agency to classify, or refer for employment any individual, for a labor organization to classify its membership or to classify or refer for employment any individual, or for an employer, labor organization, or joint labor-management committee controlling apprenticeship or other training or retraining programs to admit or employ any individual in any such program, on the basis of his religion, sex, or national origin in those certain instances where religion, sex, or national origin is a bona fide occupational qualification reasonably necessary to the normal operation of that particular business or enterprise, and (2) it shall not be an unlawful employment practice for a school, college, university, or other educational institution or institution of learning to hire and employ employees of a particular religion if such school, college, university, or other educational institution or institution of learning is, in whole or in substantial part, owned, supported, controlled, or managed by a particular religion or by a particular religious corporation, association, or society, or if the curriculum of such school, college, university, or other educational institution or institution of learning is directed toward the propagation of a particular religion.

(f) As used in this subchapter, the phrase "unlawful employment practice" shall not be deemed to include any action or measure taken by an employer, labor organization, joint labor-management committee, or employment agency with respect to an individual who is a member of the Communist Party of the United States or of any other organization required to register as a Communist—action or Communist—front organization by final order of the Subversive Activities Control Board pursuant to the Subversive Activities Control Act of 1950 [50 U.S.C. 781 et seq.].

(g) Notwithstanding any other provision of this subchapter, it shall not be an unlawful employment practice for an employer to fail or refuse to hire and employ any individual for any position, for an employer to discharge any individual from any position, or for an employment agency to fail or refuse to refer any individual for employment in any position, or for a labor organization to fail or refuse to refer any individual for employment in any position, if—

(1) the occupancy of such position, or access to the premises in or upon which any part of the duties of such position is performed or is to be performed, is subject to any requirement imposed in the interest of the national security of the United States under any security program in effect pursuant to or administered under any statute of the United States or any Executive order of the President; and

(2) such individual has not fulfilled or has ceased to fulfill that requirement.

(h) Notwithstanding any other provision of this subchapter, it shall not be an unlawful employment practice for an employer to apply different standards of compensation, or different terms, conditions, or privileges of employment pursuant to a bona fide seniority or merit system, or a system which measures earnings by quantity or quality of production or to employees who work in different locations, provided that such differences are not the result of an intention to discriminate because of race, color, religion, sex, or national origin, nor shall it be an unlawful employment practice for an employer to give and to act upon the results of any professionally developed ability test provided that such test, its administration or action upon the results is not designed, intended or used to discriminate because of race, color, religion, sex or national origin. It shall not be an unlawful employment practice under this subchapter for any employer to differentiate upon the basis of sex in determining the amount of the wages or compensation paid or to be paid to employees of such employer if such differentiation is authorized by the provisions of section 206(d) of title 29 [section 6(d) of the Fair Labor Standards Act of 1938, as amended].

(i) Nothing contained in this subchapter shall apply to any business or enterprise on or near an Indian reservation with respect to any publicly announced employment practice of such business or enterprise under which a preferential treatment is given to any individual because he is an Indian living on or near a reservation.

(j) Nothing contained in this subchapter shall be interpreted to require any employer, employment agency, labor organization, or joint labor-management committee subject to this subchapter to grant preferential treatment to any individual or to any group because of the race, color, religion, sex, or national origin of such individual or group on account of an imbalance which may exist with respect to the total number or percentage of persons of any race, color, religion, sex, or national origin employed by any employer, referred or classified for employment by any employment agency or labor organization, admitted to membership or classified by any labor organization, or admitted to, or employed in, any apprenticeship or other training program, in comparison with the total number or percentage of persons of such race, color, religion, sex, or national origin in any community, State, section, or other area, or in the available work force in any community, State, section, or other area.

(k) (1) (A) An unlawful employment practice based on disparate impact is established under this title only if—

(i) a complaining party demonstrates that a respondent uses a particular employment practice that causes a disparate impact on the basis of race, color, religion, sex, or national origin and the respondent fails to demonstrate that the challenged practice is job related for the position in question and consistent with business necessity; or

(ii) the complaining party makes the demonstration described in subparagraph (C) with respect to an alternative employment practice and the respondent refuses to adopt such alternative employment practice.

(B) (i) With respect to demonstrating that a particular employment practice causes a disparate impact as described in subparagraph (A)(i), the complaining party shall demonstrate that each particular challenged employment practice causes a disparate impact, except that if the complaining party can demonstrate to the court that the elements of a respondent's decisionmaking process are not capable of separation for analysis, the decisionmaking process may be analyzed as one employment practice.

(ii) If the respondent demonstrates that a specific employment practice does not cause the disparate impact, the respondent shall not be required to demonstrate that such practice is required by business necessity.

(C) The demonstration referred to by subparagraph (A)(ii) shall be in accordance with the law as it existed on June 4, 1989, with respect to the concept of "alternative employment practice".

(2) A demonstration that an employment practice is required by business necessity may not be used as a defense against a claim of intentional discrimination under this title.

(3) Notwithstanding any other provision of this title, a rule barring the employment of an individual who currently and knowingly uses or possesses a controlled substance, as defined in schedules I and II of section 102(6) of the Controlled Substances Act (21 U.S.C. 802(6)), other than the use or possession of a drug taken under the supervision of a licensed health care professional, or any other use or possession authorized by the Controlled Substances Act [21 U.S.C. 801 et seq.] or any other provision of Federal law, shall be considered an unlawful employment practice under this title only if such rule is adopted or applied with an intent to discriminate because of race, color, religion, sex, or national origin.

(l) It shall be an unlawful employment practice for a respondent, in connection with the selection or referral of applicants or candidates for employment or promotion, to adjust the scores of, use different cutoff scores for, or otherwise alter the results of, employment related tests on the basis of race, color, religion, sex, or national origin.

(m) Except as otherwise provided in this title, an unlawful employment practice is established when the complaining party demonstrates that race, color, religion, sex, or national origin was a motivating factor for any employment practice, even though other factors also motivated the practice.

(n) (1) (A) Notwithstanding any other provision of law, and except as provided in paragraph (2), an employment practice that implements and is within the scope of a litigated or consent judgment or order that resolves a claim of employment discrimination under the Constitution or Federal civil rights laws may not be challenged under the circumstances described in subparagraph (B).

(B) A practice described in subparagraph (A) may not be challenged in a claim under the Constitution or Federal civil rights laws—

(i) by a person who, prior to the entry of the judgment or order described in subparagraph (A), had—

(I) actual notice of the proposed judgment or order sufficient to apprise such person that such judgment or order might adversely affect the interests and legal rights of such person and that an opportunity was available to present objections to such judgment or order by a future date certain; and

(II) a reasonable opportunity to present objections to such judgment or order; or

(ii) by a person whose interests were adequately represented by another person who had previously challenged the judgment or order on the same legal grounds and with a similar factual situation, unless there has been an intervening change in law or fact.

(2) Nothing in this subsection shall be construed to—

(A) alter the standards for intervention under rule 24 of the Federal Rules of Civil Procedure or apply to the rights of parties who have successfully intervened pursuant to such rule in the proceeding in which the parties intervened;

(B) apply to the rights of parties to the action in which a litigated or consent judgment or order was entered, or of members of a class represented or sought to be represented in such action, or of members of a group on whose behalf relief was sought in such action by the Federal Government;

(C) prevent challenges to a litigated or consent judgment or order on the ground that such judgment or order was obtained through collusion or fraud, or is transparently invalid or was entered by a court lacking subject matter jurisdiction; or

(D) authorize or permit the denial to any person of the due process of law required by the Constitution.

(3) Any action not precluded under this subsection that challenges an employment consent judgment or order described in paragraph (1) shall be brought in the court, and if possible before the judge, that entered such judgment or order. Nothing in this subsection shall preclude a transfer of such action pursuant to section 1404 of title 28, United States Code.

OTHER UNLAWFUL EMPLOYMENT PRACTICES

SEC. 2000e-3. [Section 704]

(a) It shall be an unlawful employment practice for an employer to discriminate against any of his employees or applicants for employment, for an employment agency, or joint labor-management committee controlling apprenticeship or other training or retraining, including on-the-job training programs, to discriminate against any individual, or for a labor organization to discriminate against any member thereof or applicant for membership, because he has opposed any practice made an unlawful employment practice by this subchapter, or because he has made a charge, testified, assisted, or participated in any manner in an investigation, proceeding, or hearing under this subchapter.

(b) It shall be an unlawful employment practice for an employer, labor organization, employment agency, or joint labor-management committee controlling apprenticeship or other training or retraining, including on-the-job training programs, to print or publish or cause to be printed or published any notice or advertisement relating to employment by such an employer or membership in or any classification or referral for employment by such a labor organization, or relating to any classification or referral for employment by such an employment agency, or relating to admission to, or employment in, any program established to provide apprenticeship or other training by such a joint labor-management committee, indicating any preference, limitation, specification, or discrimination, based on race, color, religion, sex, or national origin, except that such a notice or advertisement may indicate a preference, limitation, specification, or discrimination based on religion, sex, or national origin when religion, sex, or national origin is a bona fide occupational qualification for employment.

EQUAL EMPLOYMENT OPPORTUNITY COMMISSION

SEC. 2000e-4. [Section 705]

(a) There is hereby created a Commission to be known as the Equal Employment Opportunity Commission, which shall be composed of five members, not more than three of whom shall be members of the same political party. Members of the Commission shall be appointed by the President by and with the advice and consent of the Senate for a term of five years. Any individual chosen to fill a vacancy shall be appointed only for the unexpired term of the member whom he shall succeed, and all members of the Commission shall continue to serve until their successors are appointed and qualified, except that no such member of the Commission shall continue to serve (1) for more than sixty days when the Congress is in session unless a nomination to fill such vacancy shall have been submitted to the Senate, or (2) after the adjournment sine die of the session of the Senate in which such nomination was submitted. The President shall designate one member to serve as Chairman of the Commission, and one member to serve as Vice Chairman. The Chairman shall be responsible on behalf of the Commission for the administrative operations of the Commission, and, except as provided in subsection (b) of this section, shall appoint, in accordance with the provisions of title 5 [United States Code] governing appointments in the competitive service, such officers, agents, attorneys, administrative law judges [hearing examiners], and employees as he deems necessary to assist it in the performance of its functions and to fix their compensation in accordance with the provisions of chapter 51 and subchapter III of chapter 53 of title 5

[United States Code], relating to classification and General Schedule pay rates: Provided, That assignment, removal, and compensation of administrative law judges [hearing examiners] shall be in accordance with sections 3105, 3344, 5372, and 7521 of title 5 [United States Code].

(b) (1) There shall be a General Counsel of the Commission appointed by the President, by and with the advice and consent of the Senate, for a term of four years. The General Counsel shall have responsibility for the conduct of litigation as provided in sections 2000e-5 and 2000e-6 of this title [sections 706 and 707]. The General Counsel shall have such other duties as the Commission may prescribe or as may be provided by law and shall concur with the Chairman of the Commission on the appointment and supervision of regional attorneys. The General Counsel of the Commission on the effective date of this Act shall continue in such position and perform the functions specified in this subsection until a successor is appointed and qualified.

(2) Attorneys appointed under this section may, at the direction of the Commission, appear for and represent the Commission in any case in court, provided that the Attorney General shall conduct all litigation to which the Commission is a party in the Supreme Court pursuant to this subchapter.

(c) A vacancy in the Commission shall not impair the right of the remaining members to exercise all the powers of the Commission and three members thereof shall constitute a quorum.

(d) The Commission shall have an official seal which shall be judicially noticed.

(e) The Commission shall at the close of each fiscal year report to the Congress and to the President concerning the action it has taken [the names, salaries, and duties of all individuals in its employ] and the moneys it has disbursed. It shall make such further reports on the cause of and means of eliminating discrimination and such recommendations for further legislation as may appear desirable.

(f) The principal office of the Commission shall be in or near the District of Columbia, but it may meet or exercise any or all of its powers at any other place. The Commission may establish such regional or State offices as it deems necessary to accomplish the purpose of this subchapter.

(g) The Commission shall have power—

(1) to cooperate with and, with their consent, utilize regional, State, local, and other agencies, both public and private, and individuals;

(2) to pay to witnesses whose depositions are taken or who are summoned before the Commission or any of its agents the same witness and mileage fees as are paid to witnesses in the courts of the United States;

(3) to furnish to persons subject to this subchapter such technical assistance as they may request to further their compliance with this subchapter or an order issued thereunder;

(4) upon the request of (i) any employer, whose employees or some of them, or (ii) any labor organization, whose members or some of them, refuse or threaten to refuse to cooperate in effectuating the provisions of this subchapter, to assist in such effectuation by conciliation or such other remedial action as is provided by this subchapter;

(5) to make such technical studies as are appropriate to effectuate the purposes and policies of this subchapter and to make the results of such studies available to the public;

(6) to intervene in a civil action brought under section 2000e-5 of this title [section 706] by an aggrieved party against a respondent other than a government, governmental agency or political subdivision.

(h) (1) The Commission shall, in any of its educational or promotional activities, cooperate with other departments and agencies in the performance of such educational and promotional activities.

(2) In exercising its powers under this title, the Commission shall carry out educational and outreach activities (including dissemination of information in languages other than English) targeted to—

(A) individuals who historically have been victims of employment discrimination and have not been equitably served by the Commission; and

(B) individuals on whose behalf the Commission has authority to enforce any other law prohibiting employment discrimination, concerning rights and obligations under this title or such law, as the case may be.

(i) All officers, agents, attorneys, and employees of the Commission shall be subject to the provisions of section 7324 of title 5 [section 9 of the Act of August 2, 1939, as amended (the Hatch Act)], notwithstanding any exemption contained in such section.

(j) (1) The Commission shall establish a Technical Assistance Training Institute, through which the Commission shall provide technical assistance and training regarding the laws and regulations enforced by the Commission.

(2) An employer or other entity covered under this title shall not be excused from compliance with the requirements of this title because of any failure to receive technical assistance under this subsection.

(3) There are authorized to be appropriated to carry out this subsection such sums as may be necessary for fiscal year 1992.

ENFORCEMENT PROVISIONS

SEC. 2000e-5. [Section 706]

(a) The Commission is empowered, as hereinafter provided, to prevent any person from engaging in any unlawful employment practice as set forth in section 2000e-2 or 2000e-3 of this title [section 703 or 704].

(b) Whenever a charge is filed by or on behalf of a person claiming to be aggrieved, or by a member of the Commission, alleging that an employer, employment agency, labor organization, or joint labor-management committee controlling apprenticeship or other training or retraining, including on-the-job training programs, has engaged in an unlawful employment practice, the Commission shall serve a notice of the charge (including the date, place and circumstances of the alleged unlawful employment practice) on such employer, employment agency, labor organization, or joint labor-management committee (hereinafter referred to as the "respondent") within ten days, and shall make an investigation thereof. Charges shall be in writing under oath or affirmation and shall contain such information and be in such form as the Commission requires. Charges shall not be made public by the Commission. If the Commission determines after such investigation that there is not reasonable cause to believe that the charge is true, it shall dismiss the charge and promptly notify the person claiming to be aggrieved and the respondent of its action. In determining whether reasonable cause exists, the Commission shall accord substantial weight to final findings and orders made by State or local authorities in proceedings commenced under State or local law pursuant to the requirements of subsections (c) and (d) of this section. If the Commission determines after such investigation that there is reasonable cause to believe that the charge is true, the Commission shall endeavor to eliminate any such alleged unlawful employment practice by informal methods of conference, conciliation, and persuasion. Nothing said or done during and as a part of such informal endeavors may be made public by the Commission, its officers or employees, or used as evidence in a subsequent proceeding without the written consent of the persons concerned. Any person who makes public information in violation of this subsection shall be fined not more than $1,000 or imprisoned for not more than one year, or both. The Commission shall make its determination on reasonable cause as promptly as possible and, so far as practicable, not later than one hundred and twenty days from the filing of the charge or, where applicable under subsection (c) or (d) of this section, from the date upon which the Commission is authorized to take action with respect to the charge.

(c) In the case of an alleged unlawful employment practice occurring in a State, or political subdivision of a State, which has a State or local law prohibiting the unlawful employment practice alleged and establishing or authorizing a State or local authority to grant or seek relief from such practice or to institute criminal proceedings with respect thereto upon receiving notice thereof, no charge may be filed under subsection (a) of this section by the person aggrieved before the expiration of sixty days after proceedings have been commenced under the State or local law, unless such proceedings have been earlier terminated, provided that such sixty-day period shall be extended to one hundred and twenty days during the first year after the effective date of such State or local law. If any requirement for the commencement of such proceedings is imposed by a State or local authority other than a requirement of the filing of a written and signed statement of the facts upon which the proceeding is based, the proceeding shall be deemed to have been commenced for the purposes of this subsection at the time such statement is sent by registered mail to the appropriate State or local authority.

(d) In the case of any charge filed by a member of the Commission alleging an unlawful employment practice occurring in a State or political subdivision of a State which has a State or local law prohibiting the practice alleged and establishing or authorizing a State or local authority to grant or seek relief from such practice or to institute criminal proceedings with respect thereto upon receiving notice thereof, the Commission shall, before taking any action with respect to such charge, notify the appropriate State or local officials and, upon request, afford them a reasonable time, but not less than sixty days (provided that such sixty-day period shall be extended to one hundred and twenty days during the first year after the effective day of such State or local law), unless a shorter period is requested, to act under such State or local law to remedy the practice alleged.

(e) (1) A charge under this section shall be filed within one hundred and eighty days after the alleged unlawful employment practice occurred and notice of the charge (including the date, place and cir-

cumstances of the alleged unlawful employment practice) shall be served upon the person against whom such charge is made within ten days thereafter, except that in a case of an unlawful employment practice with respect to which the person aggrieved has initially instituted proceedings with a State or local agency with authority to grant or seek relief from such practice or to institute criminal proceedings with respect thereto upon receiving notice thereof, such charge shall be filed by or on behalf of the person aggrieved within three hundred days after the alleged unlawful employment practice occurred, or within thirty days after receiving notice that the State or local agency has terminated the proceedings under the State or local law, whichever is earlier, and a copy of such charge shall be filed by the Commission with the State or local agency.

(2) For purposes of this section, an unlawful employment practice occurs, with respect to a seniority system that has been adopted for an intentionally discriminatory purpose in violation of this title (whether or not that discriminatory purpose is apparent on the face of the seniority provision), when the seniority system is adopted, when an individual becomes subject to the seniority system, or when a person aggrieved is injured by the application of the seniority system or provision of the system.

(f) (1) If within thirty days after a charge is filed with the Commission or within thirty days after expiration of any period of reference under subsection (c) or (d) of this section, the Commission has been unable to secure from the respondent a conciliation agreement acceptable to the Commission, the Commission may bring a civil action against any respondent not a government, governmental agency, or political subdivision named in the charge. In the case of a respondent which is a government, governmental agency, or political subdivision, if the Commission has been unable to secure from the respondent a conciliation agreement acceptable to the Commission, the Commission shall take no further action and shall refer the case to the Attorney General who may bring a civil action against such respondent in the appropriate United States district court. The person or persons aggrieved shall have the right to intervene in a civil action brought by the Commission or the Attorney General in a case involving a government, governmental agency, or political subdivision. If a charge filed with the Commission pursuant to subsection (b) of this section, is dismissed by the Commission, or if within one hundred and eighty days from the filing of such charge or the expiration of any period of reference under subsection (c) or (d) of this section, whichever is later, the Commission has not filed a civil action under this section or the Attorney General has not filed a civil action in a case involving a government, governmental agency, or political subdivision, or the Commission has not entered into a conciliation agreement to which the person aggrieved is a party, the Commission, or the Attorney General in a case involving a government, governmental agency, or political subdivision, shall so notify the person aggrieved and within ninety days after the giving of such notice a civil action may be brought against the respondent named in the charge (A) by the person claiming to be aggrieved or (B) if such charge was filed by a member of the Commission, by any person whom the charge alleges was aggrieved by the alleged unlawful employment practice. Upon application by the complainant and in such circumstances as the court may deem just, the court may appoint an attorney for such complainant and may authorize the commencement of the action without the payment of fees, costs, or security. Upon timely application, the court may, in its discretion, permit the Commission, or the Attorney General in a case involving a government, governmental agency, or political subdivision, to intervene in such civil action upon certification that the case is of general public importance. Upon request, the court may, in its discretion, stay further proceedings for not more than sixty days pending the termination of State or local proceedings described in subsection (c) or (d) of this section or further efforts of the Commission to obtain voluntary compliance.

(2) Whenever a charge is filed with the Commission and the Commission concludes on the basis of a preliminary investigation that prompt judicial action is necessary to carry out the purposes of this Act, the Commission, or the Attorney General in a case involving a government, governmental agency, or political subdivision, may bring an action for appropriate temporary or preliminary relief pending final disposition of such charge. Any temporary restraining order or other order granting preliminary or temporary relief shall be issued in accordance with rule 65 of the Federal Rules of Civil Procedure. It shall be the duty of a court having jurisdiction over proceedings under this section to assign cases for hearing at the earliest practicable date and to cause such cases to be in every way expedited.

(3) Each United States district court and each United States court of a place subject to the jurisdiction of the United States shall have jurisdiction of actions brought under this subchapter. Such an action may be brought in any judicial district in the State in which the unlawful employment practice is alleged to have been committed, in the judicial district in which the employment records relevant to such practice are maintained and administered, or in the judicial district in which the aggrieved person would have worked but for the alleged unlawful employment practice, but if the respondent is not found within any such district, such an action may be brought within the judicial district in which the respondent has his principal office. For purposes of sections 1404 and 1406 of title 28

[of the United States Code], the judicial district in which the respondent has his principal office shall in all cases be considered a district in which the action might have been brought.

(4) It shall be the duty of the chief judge of the district (or in his absence, the acting chief judge) in which the case is pending immediately to designate a judge in such district to hear and determine the case. In the event that no judge in the district is available to hear and determine the case, the chief judge of the district, or the acting chief judge, as the case may be, shall certify this fact to the chief judge of the circuit (or in his absence, the acting chief judge) who shall then designate a district or circuit judge of the circuit to hear and determine the case.

(5) It shall be the duty of the judge designated pursuant to this subsection to assign the case for hearing at the earliest practicable date and to cause the case to be in every way expedited. If such judge has not scheduled the case for trial within one hundred and twenty days after issue has been joined, that judge may appoint a master pursuant to rule 53 of the Federal Rules of Civil Procedure.

(g) (1) If the court finds that the respondent has intentionally engaged in or is intentionally engaging in an unlawful employment practice charged in the complaint, the court may enjoin the respondent from engaging in such unlawful employment practice, and order such affirmative action as may be appropriate, which may include, but is not limited to, reinstatement or hiring of employees, with or without back pay (payable by the employer, employment agency, or labor organization, as the case may be, responsible for the unlawful employment practice), or any other equitable relief as the court deems appropriate. Back pay liability shall not accrue from a date more than two years prior to the filing of a charge with the Commission. Interim earnings or amounts earnable with reasonable diligence by the person or persons discriminated against shall operate to reduce the back pay otherwise allowable.

(2) (A) No order of the court shall require the admission or reinstatement of an individual as a member of a union, or the hiring, reinstatement, or promotion of an individual as an employee, or the payment to him of any back pay, if such individual was refused admission, suspended, or expelled, or was refused employment or advancement or was suspended or discharged for any reason other than discrimination on account of race, color, religion, sex, or national origin or in violation of section 2000e-3(a) of this title [section 704(a)].

(B) On a claim in which an individual proves a violation under section 2000e-2(m) of this title [section 703(m)] and a respondent demonstrates that the respondent would have taken the same action in the absence of the impermissible motivating factor, the court—

(i) may grant declaratory relief, injunctive relief (except as provided in clause (ii), and attorney's fees and costs demonstrated to be directly attributable only to the pursuit of a claim under section 2000e-2(m) of this title [section 703(m)]; and

(ii) shall not award damages or issue an order requiring any admission, reinstatement, hiring, promotion, or payment, described in subparagraph (A).

(h) The provisions of chapter 6 of title 29 [the Act entitled "An Act to amend the Judicial Code and to define and limit the jurisdiction of courts sitting in equity, and for other purposes," approved March 23, 1932 (29 U.S.C. 105-115)] shall not apply with respect to civil actions brought under this section.

(i) In any case in which an employer, employment agency, or labor organization fails to comply with an order of a court issued in a civil action brought under this section, the Commission may commence proceedings to compel compliance with such order.

(j) Any civil action brought under this section and any proceedings brought under subsection (i) of this section shall be subject to appeal as provided in sections 1291 and 1292, title 28 [United States Code].

(k) In any action or proceeding under this subchapter the court, in its discretion, may allow the prevailing party, other than the Commission or the United States, a reasonable attorney's fee (including expert fees) as part of the costs, and the Commission and the United States shall be liable for costs the same as a private person.

CIVIL ACTIONS BY THE ATTORNEY GENERAL

SEC. 2000e-6. [Section 707]

(a) Whenever the Attorney General has reasonable cause to believe that any person or group of persons is engaged in a pattern or practice of resistance to the full enjoyment of any of the rights secured by this subchapter, and that the pattern or practice is of such a nature and is intended to deny the full exercise of the rights herein described, the Attorney General may bring a civil action in the appropriate district court of the United States by filing with it a complaint (1) signed by him (or in his absence the Acting Attorney General), (2) setting forth facts pertaining to such pattern or practice, and (3) requesting such relief, including an application for a permanent or temporary injunction, restraining order or other order against the person or persons responsible for such pattern or practice, as he deems necessary to insure the full enjoyment of the rights herein described.

(b) The district courts of the United States shall have and shall exercise jurisdiction of proceedings instituted pursuant to this section, and in any such proceeding the Attorney General may file with the clerk of such court a request that a court of three judges be convened to hear and determine the case. Such request by the Attorney General shall be accompanied by a certificate that, in his opinion, the case is of general public importance. A copy of the certificate and request for a three-judge court shall be immediately furnished by such clerk to the chief judge of the circuit (or in his absence, the presiding circuit judge of the circuit) in which the case is pending. Upon receipt of such request it shall be the duty of the chief judge of the circuit or the presiding circuit judge, as the case may be, to designate immediately three judges in such circuit, of whom at least one shall be a circuit judge and another of whom shall be a district judge of the court in which the proceeding was instituted, to hear and determine such case, and it shall be the duty of the judges so designated to assign the case for hearing at the earliest practicable date, to participate in the hearing and determination thereof, and to cause the case to be in every way expedited. An appeal from the final judgment of such court will lie to the Supreme Court.

In the event the Attorney General fails to file such a request in any such proceeding, it shall be the duty of the chief judge of the district (or in his absence, the acting chief judge) in which the case is pending immediately to designate a judge in such district to hear and determine the case. In the event that no judge in the district is available to hear and determine the case, the chief judge of the district, or the acting chief judge, as the case may be, shall certify this fact to the chief judge of the circuit (or in his absence, the acting chief judge) who shall then designate a district or circuit judge of the circuit to hear and determine the case.

It shall be the duty of the judge designated pursuant to this section to assign the case for hearing at the earliest practicable date and to cause the case to be in every way expedited.

(c) Effective two years after March 24, 1972 [the date of enactment of the Equal Employment Opportunity Act of 1972], the functions of the Attorney General under this section shall be transferred to the Commission, together with such personnel, property, records, and unexpended balances of appropriations, allocations, and other funds employed, used, held, available, or to be made available in connection with such functions unless the President submits, and neither House of Congress vetoes, a reorganization plan pursuant to chapter 9 of title 5 [United States Code], inconsistent with the provisions of this subsection. The Commission shall carry out such functions in accordance with subsections (d) and (e) of this section.

(d) Upon the transfer of functions provided for in subsection (c) of this section, in all suits commenced pursuant to this section prior to the date of such transfer, proceedings shall continue without abatement, all court orders and decrees shall remain in effect, and the Commission shall be substituted as a party for the United States of America, the Attorney General, or the Acting Attorney General, as appropriate.

(e) Subsequent to March 24, 1972 [the date of enactment of the Equal Employment Opportunity Act of 1972], the Commission shall have authority to investigate and act on a charge of a pattern or practice of discrimination, whether filed by or on behalf of a person claiming to be aggrieved or by a member of the Commission. All such actions shall be conducted in accordance with the procedures set forth in section 2000e-5 of this title [section 706].

EFFECT ON STATE LAWS

SEC. 2000e-7. [Section 708]

Nothing in this subchapter shall be deemed to exempt or relieve any person from any liability, duty, penalty, or punishment provided by any present or future law of any State or political subdivision of a State, other than any such law which purports to require or permit the doing of any act which would be an unlawful employment practice under this subchapter.

INVESTIGATIONS, INSPECTIONS, RECORDS, STATE AGENCIES

SEC. 2000e-8. [Section 709]

(a) In connection with any investigation of a charge filed under section 2000e-5 of this title [section 706], the Commission or its designated representative shall at all reasonable times have access to, for the purposes of examination, and the right to copy any evidence of any person being investigated or proceeded against that relates to unlawful employment practices covered by this subchapter and is relevant to the charge under investigation.

(b) The Commission may cooperate with State and local agencies charged with the administration of State fair employment practices laws and, with the consent of such agencies, may, for the purpose of carrying out its functions and duties under this subchapter and within the limitation of funds appropriated specifically for such purpose, engage in and contribute to the cost of research and other projects of mutual interest undertaken by such agencies, and utilize the services of such agencies and their employees, and, notwithstanding any other provision of law, pay by advance or reimbursement such agencies and their employees for services rendered to assist the Commission in carrying out this subchapter. In furtherance of such cooperative efforts, the Commission may enter into written agreements with such State or local agencies and such agreements may include provisions under which the Commission shall refrain from processing a charge in any cases or class of cases specified in such agreements or under which the Commission shall relieve any person or class of persons in such State or locality from requirements imposed under this section. The Commission shall rescind any such agreement whenever it determines that the agreement no longer serves the interest of effective enforcement of this subchapter.

(c) Every employer, employment agency, and labor organization subject to this subchapter shall (1) make and keep such records relevant to the determinations of whether unlawful employment practices have been or are being committed, (2) preserve such records for such periods, and (3) make such reports therefrom as the Commission shall prescribe by regulation or order, after public hearing, as reasonable, necessary, or appropriate for the enforcement of this subchapter or the regulations or orders thereunder. The Commission shall, by regulation, require each employer, labor organization, and joint labor-management committee subject to this subchapter which controls an apprenticeship or other training program to maintain such records as are reasonably necessary to carry out the purposes of this subchapter, including, but not limited to, a list of applicants who wish to participate in such program, including the chronological order in which applications were received, and to furnish to the Commission upon request, a detailed description of the manner in which persons are selected to participate in the apprenticeship or other training program. Any employer, employment agency, labor organization, or joint labor-management committee which believes that the application to it of any regulation or order issued under this section would result in undue hardship may apply to the Commission for an exemption from the application of such regulation or order, and, if such application for an exemption is denied, bring a civil action in the United States district court for the district where such records are kept. If the Commission or the court, as the case may be, finds that the application of the regulation or order to the employer, employment agency, or labor organization in question would impose an undue hardship, the Commission or the court, as the case may be, may grant appropriate relief. If any person required to comply with the provisions of this subsection fails or refuses to do so, the United States district court for the district in which such person is found, resides, or transacts business, shall, upon application of the Commission, or the Attorney General in a case involving a government, governmental agency or political subdivision, have jurisdiction to issue to such person an order requiring him to comply.

(d) In prescribing requirements pursuant to subsection (c) of this section, the Commission shall consult with other interested State and Federal agencies and shall endeavor to coordinate its requirements with those adopted by such agencies. The Commission shall furnish upon request and without cost to any State or local agency charged with the administration of a fair employment practice law information obtained pursuant to subsection (c) of this section from any employer, employment agency, labor organization, or joint labor-management committee subject to the jurisdiction of such agency. Such information shall be furnished on condition that it not be made public by the recipient agency prior to the institution of a proceeding under State or local law involving such information. If this condition is violated by a recipient agency, the Commission may decline to honor subsequent requests pursuant to this subsection.

(e) It shall be unlawful for any officer or employee of the Commission to make public in any manner whatever any information obtained by the Commission pursuant to its authority under this section prior to the institution of any proceeding under this subchapter involving such information. Any officer or employee of the Commission who shall make public in any manner whatever any information in violation of this subsection shall be guilty, of a misdemeanor and upon conviction thereof, shall be fined not more than $1,000, or imprisoned not more than one year.

INVESTIGATORY POWERS

SEC. 2000e-9. [Section 710]

For the purpose of all hearings and investigations conducted by the Commission or its duly authorized agents or agencies, section 161 of title 29 [section 11 of the National Labor Relations Act] shall apply.

POSTING OF NOTICES; PENALTIES

SEC. 2000e-10. [Section 711]

(a) Every employer, employment agency, and labor organization, as the case may be, shall post and keep posted in conspicuous places upon its premises where notices to employees, applicants for employment, and members are customarily posted a notice to be prepared or approved by the Commission setting forth excerpts from or summaries of, the pertinent provisions of this subchapter and information pertinent to the filing of a complaint.

(b) A willful violation of this section shall be punishable by a fine of not more than $100 for each separate offense.

VETERANS' SPECIAL RIGHTS OR PREFERENCE

SEC. 2000e-11. [Section 712]

Nothing contained in this subchapter shall be construed to repeal or modify any Federal, State, territorial, or local law creating special rights or preference for veterans.

RULES AND REGULATIONS

SEC. 2000e-12. [Section 713]

(a) The Commission shall have authority from time to time to issue, amend, or rescind suitable procedural regulations to carry out the provisions of this subchapter. Regulations issued under this section shall be in conformity with the standards and limitations of subchapter II of chapter 5 of title 5 [the Administrative Procedure Act].

(b) In any action or proceeding based on any alleged unlawful employment practice, no person shall be subject to any liability or punishment for or on account of (1) the commission by such person of an unlawful employment practice if he pleads and proves that the act or omission complained of was in good faith, in conformity with, and in reliance on any written interpretation or opinion of the Commission, or (2) the failure of such person to publish and file any information required by any provision of this subchapter if he pleads and proves that he failed to publish and file such information in good faith, in conformity with the instructions of the Commission issued under this subchapter regarding the filing of such information. Such a defense, if established, shall be a bar to the action or proceeding, notwithstanding that (A) after such act or omission, such interpretation or opinion is modified or rescinded or is determined by judicial authority to be invalid or of no legal effect, or (B) after publishing or filing the description and annual reports, such publication or filing is determined by judicial authority not to be in conformity with the requirements of this subchapter.

FORCIBLY RESISTING THE COMMISSION OR ITS REPRESENTATIVES

SEC. 2000e-13. [Section 714]

The provisions of sections 111 and 1114, title 18 [United States Code], shall apply to officers, agents, and employees of the Commission in the performance of their official duties. Notwithstanding the provisions of sections 111 and 1114 of title 18

[United States Code], whoever in violation of the provisions of section 1114 of such title kills a person while engaged in or on account of the performance of his official functions under this Act shall be punished by imprisonment for any term of years or for life.

TRANSFER OF AUTHORITY

[Administration of the duties of the Equal Employment Opportunity Coordinating Council was transferred to the Equal Employment Opportunity Commission effective July 1, 1978, under the President's Reorganization Plan of 1978.]

EQUAL EMPLOYMENT OPPORTUNITY COORDINATING COUNCIL

SEC. 2000e-14. [Section 715]

[There shall be established an Equal Employment Opportunity Coordinating Council (hereinafter referred to in this section as the Council) composed of the Secretary of Labor, the Chairman of the Equal Employment Opportunity Commission, the Attorney General, the Chairman of the United States Civil Service Commission, and the Chairman of the United States Civil Rights Commission, or their respective delegates.]

The Equal Employment Opportunity Commission [Council] shall have the responsibility for developing and implementing agreements, policies and practices designed to maximize effort, promote efficiency, and eliminate conflict, competition, duplication and inconsistency among the operations, functions and jurisdictions of the various departments, agencies and branches of the Federal Government responsible for the implementation and enforcement of equal employment opportunity legislation, orders, and policies. On or before October 1 [July 1] of each year, the Equal Employment Opportunity Commission [Council] shall transmit to the President and to the Congress a report of its activities, together with such recommendations for legislative or administrative changes as it concludes are desirable to further promote the purposes of this section.

EFFECTIVE DATE

SEC. 2000e-15. [Section 716]

[(a) This title shall become effective one year after the date of its enactment.

(b) Notwithstanding subsection (a), sections of this title other than sections 703, 704, 706, and 707 shall become effective immediately.

(c)] The President shall, as soon as feasible after July 2, 1964 [the enactment of this title], convene one or more conferences for the purpose of enabling the leaders of groups whose members will be affected by this subchapter to become familiar with the rights afforded and obligations imposed by its provisions, and for the purpose of making plans which will result in the fair and effective administration of this subchapter when all of its provisions become effective. The President shall invite the participation in such conference or conferences of (1) the members of the President's Committee on Equal Employment Opportunity, (2) the members of the Commission on Civil Rights, (3) representatives of State and local agencies engaged in furthering equal employment opportunity, (4) representatives of private agencies engaged in furthering equal employment opportunity, and (5) representatives of employers, labor organizations, and employment agencies who will be subject to this subchapter.

TRANSFER OF AUTHORITY

[Enforcement of Section 717 was transferred to the Equal Employment Opportunity Commission from the Civil Service Commission (Office of Personnel Management) effective January 1, 1979 under the President's Reorganization Plan No. 1 of 1978.]

EMPLOYMENT BY FEDERAL GOVERNMENT

SEC. 2000e-16. [Section 717]

(a) All personnel actions affecting employees or applicants for employment (except with regard to aliens employed outside the limits of the United States) in military departments as defined in section 102 of title 5 [United States Code], in executive agencies [other than the General Accounting Office] as defined in section 105 of title 5 [United States Code] (including employees and applicants for employment who are paid from nonappropriated funds), in the United States Postal Service and the Postal Rate Commission, in those units of the Government of the District of Columbia having positions in the competitive service, and in those units of the legislative and judicial branches of the Federal Government having positions in the competitive service, and in the Library of Congress shall be made free from any discrimination based on race, color, religion, sex, or national origin.

(b) Except as otherwise provided in this subsection, the Equal

Employment Opportunity Commission [Civil Service Commission] shall have authority to enforce the provisions of subsection (a) of this section through appropriate remedies, including reinstatement or hiring of employees with or without back pay, as will effectuate the policies of this section, and shall issue such rules, regulations, orders and instructions as it deems necessary and appropriate to carry out its responsibilities under this section. The Equal Employment Opportunity Commission [Civil Service Commission] shall—

(1) be responsible for the annual review and approval of a national and regional equal employment opportunity plan which each department and agency and each appropriate unit referred to in subsection (a) of this section shall submit in order to maintain an affirmative program of equal employment opportunity for all such employees and applicants for employment;

(2) be responsible for the review and evaluation of the operation of all agency equal employment opportunity programs, periodically obtaining and publishing (on at least a semiannual basis) progress reports from each such department, agency, or unit; and

(3) consult with and solicit the recommendations of interested individuals, groups, and organizations relating to equal employment opportunity.

The head of each such department, agency, or unit shall comply with such rules, regulations, orders, and instructions which shall include a provision that an employee or applicant for employment shall be notified of any final action taken on any complaint of discrimination filed by him thereunder. The plan submitted by each department, agency, and unit shall include, but not be limited to—

(1) provision for the establishment of training and education programs designed to provide a maximum opportunity for employees to advance so as to perform at their highest potential; and

(2) a description of the qualifications in terms of training and experience relating to equal employment opportunity for the principal and operating officials of each such department, agency, or unit responsible for carrying out the equal employment opportunity program and of the allocation of personnel and resources proposed by such department, agency, or unit to carry out its equal employment opportunity program.

With respect to employment in the Library of Congress, authorities granted in this subsection to the Equal Employment Opportunity Commission [Civil Service Commission] shall be exercised by the Librarian of Congress.

(c) Within 90 days of receipt of notice of final action taken by a department, agency, or unit referred to in subsection (a) of this section, or by the Equal Employment Opportunity Commission [Civil Service Commission] upon an appeal from a decision or order of such department, agency, or unit on a complaint of discrimination based on race, color, religion, sex or national origin, brought pursuant to subsection (a) of this section, Executive Order 11478 or any succeeding Executive orders, or after one hundred and eighty days from the filing of the initial charge with the department, agency, or unit or with the Equal Employment Opportunity Commission [Civil Service Commission] on appeal from a decision or order of such department, agency, or unit until such time as final action may be taken by a department, agency, or unit, an employee or applicant for employment, if aggrieved by the final disposition of his complaint, or by the failure to take final action on his complaint, may file a civil action as provided in section 2000e-5 of this title [section 706], in which civil action the head of the department, agency, or unit, as appropriate, shall be the defendant.

(d) The provisions of section 2000e-5(f) through (k) of this title [section 706(f) through (k)], as applicable, shall govern civil actions brought hereunder, and the same interest to compensate for delay in payment shall be available as in cases involving nonpublic parties.

(e) Nothing contained in this Act shall relieve any Government agency or official of its or his primary responsibility to assure nondiscrimination in employment as required by the Constitution and statutes or of its or his responsibilities under Executive Order 11478 relating to equal employment opportunity in the Federal Government.

SPECIAL PROVISIONS WITH RESPECT TO DENIAL, TERMINATION, AND SUSPENSION OF GOVERNMENT CONTRACTS

SEC. 2000e-17. [Section 718]

No Government contract, or portion thereof, with any employer, shall be denied, withheld, terminated, or suspended, by any agency or officer of the United States under any equal employment opportunity law or order, where such employer has an affirmative action plan which has previously been accepted by the Government for the same facility within the past twelve months without first according such employer full hearing and adjudication under the provisions of section 554 of title 5 [United States Code], and the following pertinent sections: Provided, That if such employer has deviated substantially from such previously agreed to affirmative action plan, this section shall not apply: Provided further, That for the purposes of this section an affirmative action plan shall be deemed to have been accepted by the Government at the time the appropriate compliance agency has accepted such plan unless within forty-five days thereafter the Office of Federal Contract Compliance has disapproved such plan.

Voting Rights Act of 1965

United States Code

Title 42—The Public Health and Welfare

Chapter 20—Elective Franchise

Subchapter I—Generally

Sec. 1971. Voting rights

(a) Race, color, or previous condition not to affect right to vote; uniform standards for voting qualifications; errors or omissions from papers; literacy tests; agreements between Attorney General and State or local authorities; definitions

(1) All citizens of the United States who are otherwise qualified by law to vote at any election by the people in any State, Territory, district, county, city, parish, township, school district, municipality, or other territorial subdivision, shall be entitled and allowed to vote at all such elections, without distinction of race, color, or previous condition of servitude; any constitution, law, custom, usage, or regulation of any State or Territory, or by or under its authority, to the contrary notwithstanding.

(2) No person acting under color of law shall—

(A) in determining whether any individual is qualified under State law or laws to vote in any election, apply any standard, practice, or procedure different from the standards, practices, or procedures applied under such law or laws to other individuals within the same county, parish, or similar political subdivision who have been found by State officials to be qualified to vote;

(B) deny the right of any individual to vote in any election because of an error or omission on any record or paper relating to any application, registration, or other act requisite to voting, if such error or omission is not material in determining whether such individual is qualified under State law to vote in such election; or

(C) employ any literacy test as a qualification for voting in any election unless (i) such test is administered to each individual and is conducted wholly in writing, and (ii) a certified copy of the test and of the answers given by the individual is furnished to him within twenty-five days of the submission of his request made within the period of time during which records and papers are required to be retained and preserved pursuant to title III of the Civil Rights Act of 1960 (42 U.S.C. 1974 et seq.): Provided, however, That the Attorney General may enter into agreements with appropriate State or local authorities that preparation, conduct, and maintenance of such tests in accordance with the provisions of applicable State or local law, including such special provisions as are necessary in the preparation, conduct, and maintenance of such tests for persons who are blind or otherwise physically handicapped, meet the purposes of this subparagraph and constitute compliance therewith.

(3) For purposes of this subsection—

(A) the term "vote" shall have the same meaning as in subsection (e) of this section;

(B) the phrase "literacy test" includes any test of the ability to read, write, understand, or interpret any matter.

(b) Intimidation, threats, or coercion

No person, whether acting under color of law or otherwise, shall intimidate, threaten, coerce, or attempt to intimidate, threaten, or coerce any other person for the purpose of interfering with the right of such other person to vote or to vote as he may choose, or of causing such other person to vote for, or not to vote for, any candidate for the office of President, Vice President, presidential elector, Member of the Senate, or Member of the House of Representatives, Delegates or Commissioners from the Territories or possessions, at any general, special, or primary election held solely or in part for the purpose of selecting or electing any such candidate.

(c) Preventive relief; injunction; rebuttable literacy presumption;

liability of United States for costs; State as party defendant

Whenever any person has engaged or there are reasonable grounds to believe that any person is about to engage in any act or practice which would deprive any other person of any right or privilege secured by subsection (a) or (b) of this section, the Attorney General may institute for the United States, or in the name of the United States, a civil action or other proper proceeding for preventive relief, including an application for a permanent or temporary injunction, restraining order, or other order. If in any such proceeding literacy is a relevant fact there shall be a rebuttable presumption that any person who has not been adjudged an incompetent and who has completed the sixth grade in a public school in, or a private school accredited by, any State or territory, the District of Columbia, or the Commonwealth of Puerto Rico where instruction is carried on predominantly in the English language, possesses sufficient literacy, comprehension, and intelligence to vote in any election. In any proceeding hereunder the United States shall be liable for costs the same as a private person. Whenever, in a proceeding instituted under this subsection any official of a State or subdivision thereof is alleged to have committed any act or practice constituting a deprivation of any right or privilege secured by subsection (a) of this section, the act or practice shall also be deemed that of the State and the State may be joined as a party defendant and, if, prior to the institution of such proceeding, such official has resigned or has been relieved of his office and no successor has assumed such office, the proceeding may be instituted against the State.

(d) Jurisdiction; exhaustion of other remedies

The district courts of the United States shall have jurisdiction of proceedings instituted pursuant to this section and shall exercise the same without regard to whether the party aggrieved shall have exhausted any administrative or other remedies that may be provided by law.

(e) Order qualifying person to vote; application; hearing; voting referees; transmittal of report and order; certificate of qualification; definitions

In any proceeding instituted pursuant to subsection (c) of this section in the event the court finds that any person has been deprived on account of race or color of any right or privilege secured by subsection (a) of this section, the court shall upon request of the Attorney General and after each party has been given notice and the opportunity to be heard make a finding whether such deprivation was or is pursuant to a pattern or practice. If the court finds such pattern or practice, any person of such race or color resident within the affected area shall, for one year and thereafter until the court subsequently finds that such pattern or practice has ceased, be entitled, upon his application therefor, to an order declaring him qualified to vote, upon proof that at any election or elections (1) he is qualified under State law to vote, and (2) he has since such finding by the court been (a) deprived of or denied under color of law the opportunity to register to vote or otherwise to qualify to vote, or (b) found not qualified to vote by any person acting under color of law. Such order shall be effective as to any election held within the longest period for which such applicant could have been registered or otherwise qualified under State law at which the applicant's qualifications would under State law entitle him to vote.

Notwithstanding any inconsistent provision of State law or the action of any State officer or court, an applicant so declared qualified to vote shall be permitted to vote in any such election. The Attorney General shall cause to be transmitted certified copies of such order to the appropriate election officers. The refusal by any such officer with notice of such order to permit any person so declared qualified to vote to vote at an appropriate election shall constitute con-tempt of court. An application for an order pursuant to this subsection shall be heard within ten days, and the execution of any order disposing of such application shall not be stayed if the effect of such stay would be to delay the effectiveness of the order beyond the date of any election at which the applicant would otherwise be enabled to vote.

The court may appoint one or more persons who are qualified voters in the judicial district, to be known as voting referees, who shall subscribe to the oath of office required by section 3331 of title 5, to serve for such period as the court shall determine, to receive such applications and to take evidence and report to the court findings as to whether or not at any election or elections

(1) any such applicant is qualified under State law to vote, and

(2) he has since the finding by the court heretofore specified been

(a) deprived of or denied under color of law the opportunity to register to vote or otherwise to qualify to vote, or (b) found not qualified to vote by any person acting under color of law. In a proceeding before a voting referee, the applicant shall be heard *ex parte* at such times and places as the court shall direct. His statement under oath shall be *prima facie* evidence as to his age, residence, and his prior efforts to register or otherwise qualify to vote. Where proof of literacy or an understanding of other subjects is required by valid provisions of State law, the answer of the applicant, if written, shall be included in such report to the court; if oral, it shall be taken down stenographically and a transcription included in such report to the court.

Upon receipt of such report, the court shall cause the Attorney General to transmit a copy thereof to the State attorney general and to each party to such proceeding together with an order to show cause within ten days, or such shorter time as the court may fix, why an order of the court should not be entered in accordance with such report. Upon the expiration of such period, such order shall be entered unless prior to that time there has been filed with the court and served upon all parties a statement of exceptions to such report. Exceptions as to matters of fact shall be considered only if supported by a duly verified copy of a public record or by affidavit of persons having personal knowledge of such facts or by statements or matters contained in such report; those relating to matters of law shall be supported by an appropriate memorandum of law. The issues of fact and law raised by such exceptions shall be determined by the court or, if the due and speedy administration of justice requires, they may be referred to the voting referee to determine in accordance with procedures prescribed by the court. A hearing as to an issue of fact shall be held only in the event that the proof in support of the exception disclose the existence of a genuine issue of material fact. The applicant's literacy and understanding of other subjects shall be determined solely on the basis of answers included in the report of the voting referee.

The court, or at its direction the voting referee, shall issue to each applicant so declared qualified a certificate identifying the holder thereof as a person so qualified.

Any voting referee appointed by the court pursuant to this subsection shall to the extent not inconsistent herewith have all the powers conferred upon a master by rule 53(c) of the Federal Rules of Civil Procedure. The compensation to be allowed to any persons appointed by the court pursuant to this subsection shall be fixed by the court and shall be payable by the United States.

Applications pursuant to this subsection shall be determined expeditiously. In the case of any application filed twenty or more days prior to an election which is undetermined by the time of such election, the court shall issue an order authorizing the applicant to vote provisionally: Provided, however, That such applicant shall be qualified to vote under State law. In the case of an application filed within twenty days prior to an election, the court, in its discretion, may make such an order. In either case the order shall make appropriate provision for the impounding of the applicant's ballot pending determination of the application. The court may take any other action, and may authorize such referee or such other person as it may designate to take any other action, appropriate or necessary to carry out the provisions of this subsection and to enforce its decrees. This subsection shall in no way be construed as a limitation upon the existing powers of the court.

When used in the subsection, the word "vote" includes all action necessary to make a vote effective including, but not limited to, registration or other action required by State law prerequisite to voting, casting a ballot, and having such ballot counted and included in the appropriate totals of votes cast with respect to candidates for public office and propositions for which votes are received in an election; the words "affected area" shall mean any subdivision of the State in which the laws of the State relating to voting are or have been to any extent administered by a person found in the proceeding to have violated subsection (a) of this section; and the words "qualified under State law" shall mean qualified according to the laws, customs, or usages of the State, and shall not, in any event, imply qualifications more stringent than those used by the persons found in the proceeding to have violated subsection (a) in qualifying persons other than those of the race or color against which the pattern or practice of discrimination was found to exist.

(f) Contempt; assignment of counsel; witnesses

Any person cited for an alleged contempt under this Act shall be allowed to make his full defense by counsel learned in the law; and the court before which he is cited or tried, or some judge thereof, shall immediately, upon his request, assign to him such counsel, not exceeding two, as he may desire, who shall have free access to him at all reasonable hours. He shall be allowed, in his defense to make any proof that he can produce by lawful witnesses, and shall have the like process of the court to compel his witnesses to appear at his trial or hearing, as is usually granted to compel witnesses to appear on behalf of the prosecution. If such person shall be found by the court to be financially unable to provide for such counsel, it shall be the duty of the court to provide such counsel.

(g) Three-judge district court: hearing, determination, expedition

of action, review by Supreme Court; single-judge district

court: hearing, determination, expedition of action

In any proceeding instituted by the United States in any district court of the United States under this section in which the Attorney General requests a finding of a pattern or practice of discrimination pursuant to subsection (e) of this section the Attorney General, at the time he files the complaint, or any defendant in the proceeding, within twenty days after service upon him of the complaint, may file with the clerk of such court a request that a court of three judges be convened to hear and determine the entire case. A copy of the request for a three-judge court shall be immediately furnished by such clerk to the chief judge of the circuit (or in his absence, the presiding circuit judge of the circuit) in which the case is pending. Upon receipt of the copy of such request it shall be the duty of the chief judge of the circuit or the presiding circuit judge, as the case may be, to designate immediately three judges in such circuit, of whom at least one shall be a circuit judge and another of whom shall be a district judge of the court in which the proceeding was instituted, to hear and determine such case, and it shall be the duty of the judges so designated to assign the case for hearing at the earliest practicable date, to participate in the hearing and determination thereof, and to cause the case to be in every way expedited. An appeal from the final judgment of such court will lie to the Supreme Court.

In any proceeding brought under subsection (c) of this section to enforce subsection (b) of this section, or in the event neither the Attorney General nor any defendant files a request for a three-judge court in any proceeding authorized by this subsection, it shall be the duty of the chief judge of the district (or in his absence, the acting chief judge) in which the case is pending immediately to designate a judge in such district to hear and determine the case. In the event that no judge in the district is available to hear and determine the case, the chief judge of the district, or the acting chief judge, as the case may be, shall certify this fact to the chief judge of the circuit (or, in his absence, the acting chief judge) who shall then designate a district or circuit judge of the circuit to hear and determine the case.

It shall be the duty of the judge designated pursuant to this section to assign the case for hearing at the earliest practicable date and to cause the case to be in every way expedited.

Additional Resources

If you would like to learn more about civil rights and the movements for civil rights in the past and today, this list of resources will give you places to begin.

Web Sites for Young People

The Civil Rights Movement 1955–1965
Web site www.watson.org/~lisa/blackhistory/civil-rights-55-65

Civil Rights Team Web Page
Web site www.state.me.us/ag/crt/crt.htm

Department of Justice Web Page for Children
Web site www.usdoj.gov/kidspage/bias-k-5/index.htm

Human Rights Web
Web site www.hrweb.org/

YouthPeace
Web site www.nonviolence.org

Organizations

Anacostia Museum
Smithsonian Institution
1901 Fort Place SE
Washington, DC 20020
Phone (202) 287-3369
Web site www.si.edu/organiza/museums/anacost/start.htm

Anti-Defamation League of B'nai B'rith
823 United Nations Plaza
New York, NY 10017
Phone (212) 490-2525
Fax (212) 867-0779

E-mail adl@pipeline.com
Web site www.adl.org

Center for Constitutional Rights
666 Broadway
New York, NY 10012
Phone (212) 614-6464

Children's Defense Fund
25 E Street NW
Washington, DC 20001
Phone (202) 628-8787
Fax (202) 662-3781
Web site www.childrensdefense.org/

Highlander Research and Education Center
1959 Highlander Way
New Market, TN 37820
Phone (423) 933-3443
Fax (423) 933-3424
E-mail hrec@igc.apc.org

Martin Luther King, Jr. National Historic Site
526 Auburn Avenue NE
Atlanta, GA 30312
Phone (404) 331-3919

Mexican American Legal Defense and Educational Fund
634 South Spring Street, 11th Floor
Los Angeles, CA 90014
Phone (213) 629-2512
Fax (213) 629-8016

National Association for the Advancement of Colored People (NAACP)
4805 Mount Hope Drive
Baltimore, MD 21215

Phone (410) 358-8900
Fax (410) 486-9255

National Civil Rights Museum
450 Mulberry Street
Memphis, TN 38103
Phone (901) 561-9699
Web site www.mecca.org/~crights/

National Gay and Lesbian Task Force (NGLTF)
1700 Kalorama Road, NW
Washington, DC 20009-2624
Phone (202) 332-6483
Fax (202) 332-0207
E-mail ngltf@ngltf.org
Web site www.ngltf.org

National Organization for Women (NOW)
1000 16th Street, NW, Suite 700
Washington, DC 20036
Phone (202) 331-0066
Fax (202) 785-8576
E-mail now@now.org
Web site www.now.org

National Rainbow Push Coalition
930 E. 50th Street
Chicago, IL 60615-2702
Phone (773) 373-3366
Fax (773) 373-3571
Web site www.rainbowpush.org/

Southern Christian Leadership Conference (SCLC)
334 Auburn Ave, NE
Atlanta, GA 30303
Phone (404) 522-1420
Fax (404) 659-7390

Southern Poverty Law Center (SPLC)
Box 548, 400 Washington Avenue
Montgomery, AL 36104
Phone (334) 264-0286
Fax (334) 264-0629
Web site www.splcenter.org

Videos

The videos listed in the first group tell stories of race, prejudice, and overcoming discrimination. Most are theatrical releases that will be available in video stores.

A Dry, White Season shows the recent history of apartheid in South Africa through the eyes of a white journalist who is the friend of a black activist.

El Norte is the story of two Guatemalan teens, a brother and sister fleeing the people who have killed their father. This gritty, realistic story shows that even the promised land of America has shortcomings.

Four Little Girls, a documentary produced by Spike Lee, focuses on the Civil Rights Movement in Birmingham and the events leading up to the 1963 church bombing.

Gandhi is the story of a leader who both developed and practiced nonviolent resistance to unjust laws that became the moving philosophy of Dr. Martin Luther King, Jr., in the United States. This epic movie follows Gandhi from his young adulthood in South Africa through his nonviolent leadership of the struggle for India's independence and ultimately to his death at the hands of an assassin.

A Gentleman's Agreement and *Guess Who's Coming to Dinner* are two older movies about prejudice. The "gentleman's agreement" discriminates against Jews, and the surprise dinner guest is the African American fiancé of a white woman, coming to meet her parents and their prejudices.

Hoop Dreams is a documentary record of the lives of two young African American men from Chicago's inner city. Each of them hopes that basketball will be a ticket out of poverty. The obstacles that they face include the manipulation of their hopes and their talents by college and professional basketball systems.

Malcolm X traces Malcolm's life from the poverty and racism he endured as a child through his teenage crime and imprisonment, his conversion to Islam, and his eventual movement beyond Elijah Muhammad's black separatism to his assassination.

Matewan shows the struggle of workers in the United States trying to gain recognition for their unions and protection for their rights.

The Milagro Beanfield War shows the daily life of a poor, rural Mexican American community as people struggle to maintain control of their land. Realism and magic combine in this joyful, contemporary story.

Mississippi Burning has been criticized for showing the FBI in an overly flattering light. While that criticism is accurate, the movie is valuable for its true stories of the murder of three young civil rights workers, the burning of churches, and the violent opposition to the Civil Rights Movement in Mississippi in the 1960s.

Roots is based on a book by Alex Haley, which traces his own family roots from twentieth-century United States back to Africa. The richness of African culture, the cruelty of slavery, and the strength of African American families are evident in this powerful drama. When *Roots* was broadcast as a television series in 1987, it drew wide audiences and inspired a surge of interest in family histories among people of all ethnic backgrounds.

Shoah uses actual film footage from the 1940s and interviews with Holocaust survivors to tell the story of the Nazi genocide of the Jewish people. Shoah was made so that no one could deny the reality of the Holocaust. People who lived near the death camps are interviewed as well.

Sounder is the story of an African American family living in the rural South in the mid-twentieth century. When the father is jailed, the mother quietly and courageously keeps the family together, with consistent and important help from her children. The family suffers from both poverty and racial discrimination.

Videos for Young Children

The videos listed in this group are suitable for younger elementary-school children. Some will be available in video stores. They are also generally lower-priced, and families may want to purchase them for home viewing or to donate to school or public libraries.

In *Follow the Drinking Gourd*, Morgan Freeman introduces your family to an African American family suffering under slavery in the 1800s. The heroine is a brave little girl who loves to learn and tell stories, a friend sure to appeal to preschool through early elementary school children. Although the harshness and evils of slavery may seem like difficult topics for this age group, the story offers hope that evil can be overcome and that children can help to do so (book also available).

While these stories are suitable for younger children, they are still high-interest stories that grown-ups can enjoy, too!

And the Children Shall Lead shows black and white southern children struggling with racism in the 1960s. (Wonderworks Video)

Brother Future takes a contemporary teenager on a trip in time back to the 1850s and slavery. (Wonderworks Video)

Follow the Drinking Gourd shows a young girl and her family escaping from slavery by traveling on the Underground Railroad. (Rabbit Ears Video)

Hiroshima Maiden challenges a young boy to overcome the anti-Japanese prejudices of his friends when his family opens their home to a victim of the Hiroshima atom bomb. (Wonderworks Video)

John Henry is a mythical African American hero whose strength was greater than that of the machine brought in to replace human railroad workers. (Rabbit Ears Video)

Journey to Spirit Island introduces a contemporary Indian family in the Pacific Northwest. Children triumph in the battle between greed and tradition.

The Songhai Princess is a smart and beautiful princess who has to contend with a wicked witch. The entrancing tale of Princess Nzinga introduces young viewers to the grand cities and universities of Songhai, the ancestral home of African Americans.

Spirit Rider takes Jesse, a teenage Ojibway boy, from an urban foster home to the reservation home of his grandfather, who has just been released from prison. Jesse struggles with rural life, with belonging to a family and a tribe, and with growing up, as well as with the mystery of his past. (Wonderworks Video)

Squanto and the First Thanksgiving shows Squanto's capture and enslavement by Europeans, his return to find his whole village destroyed, and the help he gives to the starving English immigrants.

Sweet 15 is the story of a Mexican American girl as she grows up. Some of the issues she faces seem universal: protective parents, friendship, and learning to work in the world. Marta also faces special problems because of her father's immigration status. (Wonderworks Video)

In addition, Schlessinger Media produces the American Cultures for Children series, which includes Arab American Heritage, Central American Heritage, Chinese American Heritage, Irish American Heritage, Japanese American Heritage, Jewish American Heritage, Korean American Heritage, Mexican American Heritage, Native American Heritage, Puerto Rican Heritage, and Vietnamese American Heritage. Schlessinger's Holidays for Children series focuses on 16 holidays, ranging from St. Patrick's Day to Ramadan. The Schlessinger series are aimed at children from kindergarten through fourth grade, but older and younger viewers will also enjoy them. Call (800) 843-3620 for catalog and to order videos.

Children's Books for Further Reading

Bridges, Ruby. *Through My Eyes*. New York: Scholastic Press, 1999.

Clark, Septima, with Cynthia Stokes Brown. *Ready from Within: A First Person Narrative*. Lawrenceville, N.J.: Africa World Press, 1990.

Coles, Robert. *The Story of Ruby Bridges*. New York: Scholastic, 1995.

Colman, Penny. *Fannie Lou Hamer and the Fight for the Vote*. Brookfield, Conn.: Millbrook Press, 1994.

Cwiklik, Robert. *A. Philip Randolph and the Labor Movement*. Brookfield, Conn.: Millbrook Press, 1994.

Darby, Jean. *Martin Luther King, Jr.* Minneapolis, Minn.: Lerner Publications, 1990.

Evers-Williams, Myrlie with Melinda Blau (contributor). *Watch Me Fly: What I Learned on the Way to Becoming the Woman I Was Meant to Be*. New York: Little, Brown & Company, 1999.

Halberstam, David. *The Children*. New York: Random House, 1998.

Jakoubek, Robert E. *James Farmer and the Freedom Rides*. Brookfield, Conn.: Millbrook Press, 1994.

King, Casey and Linda Barrett Osborne. *Oh, Freedom!* New York: Alfred A. Knopf, 1997.

Lewis, John. *Walking with the Wind: A Memoir of the Movement*. New York: Simon & Schuster, 1998.

Parks, Rosa, with Jim Haskins. *Rosa Parks: My Story*. New York: Dial Books, 1992.

Rennert, Richard. *Profiles of Great Black American Female Leaders*. New York: Chelsea House Publishers, 1994.

Siegel, Beatrice. *Marian Wright Edelman: The Making of a Crusader*. New York: Simon & Schuster, 1995.

Simon, Charman. *Jesse Jackson: I Am Somebody*. Danbury, Conn.: Children's Press, 1997.

Bibliography

Books

Branch, Taylor. *Parting the Waters: America in the King Years, 1954–63.* New York: Simon & Schuster, 1988.

Branch, Taylor. *Pillar of Fire: America in the King Years, 1963–1965.* New York: Simon & Schuster, 1998.

Clark, Septima, with Cynthia Stokes Brown. *Ready from Within: A First Person Narrative.* Lawrenceville, N.J.: Africa World Press, 1990.

Evers-Williams, Myrlie with Melinda Blau. *Watch Me Fly: What I Learned on the Way to Becoming the Woman I Was Meant to Be.* New York: Little, Brown & Company, 1999.

Halberstam, David. *The Children.* New York: Random House, 1998.

King, Casey, and Linda Barrett Osborne. *Oh, Freedom!* New York: Alfred A. Knopf, 1997.

King, Coretta Scott. *My Life with Martin Luther King, Jr.* New York: Henry Holt, 1969.

King, Martin Luther, Jr. *Stride Toward Freedom.* New York: Harper & Brothers, 1964.

King, Martin Luther, Jr. *Why We Can't Wait.* New York: Harper & Row, 1963.

Kluger, Richard. *Simple Justice.* New York: Random House, 1977.

Kozol, Jonathan. *Death at an Early Age: The Destruction of the Hearts and Minds of Negro Children in the Boston Public Schools.* Boston: Houghton Mifflin, 1967.

Malcolm X. *The Autobiography of Malcolm X, As Told to Alex Haley.* New York: Grove Press, 1964.

Mills, Kay. *This Little Light of Mine: The Life of Fannie Lou Hamer.* New York: Dutton, 1993.

Oates, Stephen B. *Let the Trumpet Sound: The Life of Martin Luther King, Jr.* New York: NAL Penguin, 1982.

Parks, Rosa, with Jim Haskins. *Rosa Parks: My Story.* New York: Dial Books, 1992.

Rennert, Richard. *Profiles of Great Black American Female Leaders.* New York: Chelsea House Publishers, 1994.

"The Status of Education in Black America, Volume II: Preschool through High School Education." Released June 1997 by the Frederick D. Patterson Research Institute of the College Fund/United Negro College Fund.

Articles

"High Court Bans School Segregation; 9-to-0 Decision Grants Time to Comply; 1896 Ruling Upset; 'Separate but Equal' Doctrine Held Out of Place in Education; High Court Bans Public Pupil Bias," Luther A. Huston. *New York Times,* 18 May 1954.

"Blast Kills Four Children; Riots Follow; Two Youths Slain; State Reinforces Birmingham Police," United Press International (UPI), 16 September 1963.

"The Algebra Project: Organizing in the Spirit of Ella," Robert Moses, Mieko Kamii, Susan McAllister Swap, and Jeffrey Howard. *Harvard Educational Review* Vol. 59, No. 4 (November 1989): 423-43.

"Passing the Torch? The New Generation of Student Activists," speech by Julian Bond. Reprinted in *The Black Collegian Magazine,* 1997. As seen on the Web at www.black-collegian.com/bond.html.

"We Stood Up at the March—A Memoir," David C. Ruffin. *FOCUS*, Monthly Public Policy Publication of the Joint Center for Political and Economic Studies, August 1998.

"African American Men Still Lag Behind White Men in Earnings; A Study Finds a College-Educated African American Man Makes on Average $13,000 Less Annually than a White College-Educated Man," Gwenda Richards Oshiro. *The Oregonian*, 24 February 1999.

"Four Decades of Progress . . . and Decline: An Assessment of African American Educational Attainment," Antoine M. Garibaldi, Howard University. The 1997 Charles H. Thompson Lecture-Colloquium Presentation. *Journal of Negro Education*. Vol. 66, No. 2 (1997).

"Southern Culture Reviews—'And Gently He Shall Lead Them: Robert Parris Moses and Civil Rights in Mississippi,' By Eric R. Burner." Brian Ward. New York University Press, 1994. *Southern Cultures*, Volume 2: Number 3/4. Fall/Winter 1996.

"Crucial Conversations," by David Ruenzel. *Teaching Tolerance* magazine, Southern Poverty Law Center, Spring 1997.

"King's eldest son to lead civil-rights group," by Chelsea J. Carter. *The Seattle Times*, 2 November 1997.

"Jesse Jackson," *Frontline* WGBH Educational Foundation New Content. PBS and WGBH/Frontline, 1998.

Web Sites

"The Civil Rights Movement 1955-1965." A history of the civil rights movement created by Lisa Cozzens. www.watson.org/~lisa/blackhistory/civil-rights-55-65.

"A Class of One: An interview of Ruby Bridges Hall," conducted by Charlayne Hunter-Gault on 18 February 1997. www.pbs.org/newshour/bb/race_relations/jan-june97/bridges_2-18.html.

"An Interview of Reverend Bernice King, the Daughter of Martin Luther King, Jr.," by Charlayne Hunter-Gault on 15 January 1997. www.pbs.org/newshour/bb/race_relations/jan-june97/king_1-15.html.

Maine Attorney General's Civil Rights Team Project. www.state.me.us/ag/crt/crt.htm.

Department of Justice Web Page for Kids www.usdoj.gov/kidspage/bias-k-5/index.htm.

National Women's Hall of Fame. Short biographies from the 1998 National Women's Hall of Fame, including Rosa Parks, Ella Baker, Fannie Lou Hamer, and Barbara Jordan. www.greatwomen.org.

Eyes on the Prize. On-line summary of six-part PBS television series on the Civil Rights Movement from 1954 to 1965. First aired on PBS in 1986. http://breakthrough.blackside.com/blackside/EducationOutreach/eyes1-guide.html [Note: This is available from PBS Video at (800) 424-7963.]

"Will the Circle Be Unbroken? A Personal History of the Civil Rights Movement in Five Southern Communities." Broadcast on National Public Radio. Southern Regional Council. www.unbrokencircle.org/

Nonviolent Civil Disobedience Handbook. "History of Mass Nonviolent Action." Fen Labalme, 1993, 1998. www.activism.net/peace/nvcdh

Watkins, Hollis. "Movement Voices: Overcoming Fear in Mississippi." ACLU, 1997. http://users.aol.com/mcluf/hollison.htm. 2 November 1999.

YouthPeace, a site with links to and information on organizations and activities focused on nonviolence. www.nonviolence.org.

Human Rights Web, a site with links to and information on organizations focused on human rights. www.hrweb.org/.

ZNet Articles on Line, links to on-line articles on race and racism, civil rights, and other multicultural topics. www.lbbs.org/multicultideas.htm.

Southern Oral History Program, links to interviews by the Southern Oral History Program. www.unc.edu/depts/sohp/SOHPweb/civilrightsproject.

More Hands-On Learning from Chicago Review Press

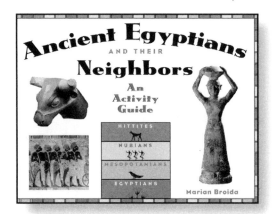

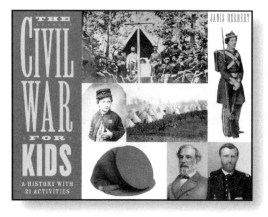

Ancient Egyptians and Their Neighbors
An Activity Guide
Marian Broida

Foreword by Gary Beckman, Professor of Hittite and Mesopotamian Studies, University of Michigan

Chosen for Smithsonian's Notable Books for Children, 1999

This activity book shows what life was like among the Nubians, Mesopotamians, Hittites, and Egyptians from around 3100 B.C., when Upper and Lower Egypt became one kingdom, to the death of Queen Cleopatra under the Romans, in 30 B.C.

ages 9 & up, 144 pages, 11 x 8½
25 b & w photos, illustrated throughout,
2-color interior
paper, $16.95 1-55652-360-2

The Civil War for Kids
A History with 21 Activities
Janis Herbert

Activities such as making butternut dye for a Rebel uniform, learning flag signals, decoding wigwag, baking hardtack, reenacting battles, and making a medicine kit bring this pivotal period in our nation's history to life.

ages 9 & up, 224 pages, 11 x 8½
50 b & w photos
paper, $14.95 1-55652-355-6

Math Games and Activities from Around the World
Claudia Zaslavsky

From the author of *Multicultural Math*

More than 70 math games, puzzles, and projects from all over the world are included in this delightful book for kids who think math is boring.

ages 8 & up, 160 pages, 11 x 8½
10 b & w photos, line drawings throughout
paper, $14.95 1-55652-287-8

These books are available from your local bookstore or from Independent Publishers Group by calling (312) 337-0747 or (800) 888-4741.